How to Grow, Employ and Transfer (GET) Wealth

How to Grow, Employ and Transfer (GET) Wealth

HENRY S. WOLOSON

Cover by City Beautiful Design

Proofreading by Stephen Tackitt

Editing by Angele Okonski

1 2 3 4 5 6 7 8 9 10

DEDICATION

To the strong women in my family who have encouraged me to reach for ever higher goals:

Diane (Spouse)

Laura (Daughter)

Katherine (Daughter)

Ines (Mother)

Carmela DeAngelis Marinelli (Nonna)

Names: Woloson, Henry, 1952 -author

Title: How to Grow, Employ and Transfer (GET) Wealth

Identifiers:

Table of Contents

PREFACE

Although learning how to manage money is a lifelong project for most people, "How to Grow, Employ and Transfer (GET) Wealth" could be especially important if you belong to one of the following groups: 1) Younger individuals interested in learning basic financial concepts that will help you better manage your future earnings and expenses; 2) Older individuals seeking a broad overview of financial management while looking for practical suggestions to enhance your wealth; and 3) People who have been hurt economically by COVID 19 and want to repair the financial damage they have experienced while preparing themselves for future financial shockwaves.

Students have a critical need to become financially literate. Those of you heading to college or are already attending college need to understand the high cost of education. Once you have a full-time job, you should know how to save money and how to make money work harder for you.

If you are more established, this book can provide a broad overview of financial management concepts. After you turn 30, financial matters like home buying and even planning for a distant retirement becomes of crucial importance. Plus, the chapters on transferring wealth are critical not only you but to your parents as well. Making sure they have effective life-plans (not just estate plans) is frequently one of the best gifts you can give your older family members.

People who have been economically injured by COVID 19 need to realize that while you have been dealt a bad hand, you are certainly not alone. At one point in 2020, over 25 million people in the United States were unemployed, many due to COVID 19- related shutdowns of business. This book discusses how to establish an Emergency Savings Account (ESA) to be better prepared when (not if) another financial storm hits.

While there is no question that many Americans have suffered financially due to COVID 19, as multi-billionaire Warren Buffet has

1

said: "Never bet against the American economy." Just as the U.S. stock markets recovered within six months from the substantial downturn experienced in February 2020, we need to have confidence that better economic days are coming. Position yourself to take advantage of the opportunities that have and will come.

Education is a never-ending process. Whether you are learning financial concepts for the first time or are expanding your understanding of investing and money management, "How To Grow, Employ and Transfer (GET) Wealth" is intended to provide a foundation to become financially literate. How you choose to build on that foundation will be your choice and will help determine how much wealth you will gain, enjoy and eventually transfer.

INTRODUCTION

"An investment in education gives the best returns."
Ben Franklin

The goal of this book is to help you become financially independent. At the risk of losing those of you looking for a magic formula that will make you a billionaire in a month or less, sorry, this is not that book.

"How To Grow, Employ and Transfer (GET) Wealth" does not include a treasure map. Instead, we are going to provide information to educate you which, as Ben Franklin said, is an investment that will give you the best returns.

For the vast majority of people, becoming wealthy takes time. To GET Wealth, you need to know principles about: 1) Saving and investing money (**Grow**); 2) Making money work for you (**Employ**); and 3) Passing your wealth to others (**Transfer**). <u>Grow, Employ and Transfer (**GET**) Wealth.</u>

Mega lottery winners are among the very few who become extremely wealthy quickly. Even then, their winning lotto ticket was usually not the first one they bought and for years they probably have purchased many losers.

Super star professional athletes who receive huge contracts have spent countless hours learning and training how to play their sport. They may be young in age but old in experience.

Entertainers who pack stadiums with adoring fans usually started playing in small bars in small towns for small or no pay. A person who is labeled an overnight success has usually spent a lot of long nights learning how to become an overnight success.

As many once rich and now bankrupt celebrities and former professional athletes prove, learning to Grow, Employ and Transfer (GET) Wealth means far more than making money. You have to learn how to make your wealth grow, effectively work for you and have something left to eventually give to your loved ones and hopefully charities that you support.

"Wealth" is defined by Merriam-Webster as "all material objects that have economic utility."

According to a survey conducted by investment company Charles Schwab, you need to have a least $1.4 million in America to be considered wealthy. But if you live in parts of San Francisco, New York City or Miami, $1.4 million will barely enable you to buy housing that would be considered a tear-down eyesore in many really nice communities in America.

Not everyone can be wealthy, regardless of how you define wealth. But most people can become financially independent if they are motivated and committed to: 1) Learn; 2) Earn; and 3) Act. To quote billionaire T. Boone Pickens: "A plan without action is not a plan. It's a speech."

Your goal should be to have enough wealth ("material objects that have economic utility") so that you feel secure that you can adequately provide for yourself, your family and for those you want to support. COVID-19 has proven that becoming financially independent is the true description of being "wealthy."

Part I: How To **Grow** Wealth

*"The journey of a thousand miles
begins with a single step."*
Lao Tzu

Think of being financially independent as both a goal and a destination. You need to take a series of small steps to become financially independent but once you develop good habits, the journey becomes easier. The first step is to acquire and grow your assets.

PREVIEW OF PART I – HOW TO GROW WEALTH

Part I of this book discusses how to grow wealth by saving, investing and safeguarding assets. You need to acquire assets (save), build those assets (invest) and make sure those assets are insured (safeguard your assets).

SECTION CHAPTERS
Section One – Save
    Chapter 1 – Emergency Savings Account (ESA)
    Chapter 2 – Tax-Favored Assets
    Chapter 3 – Retirement Plans and Accounts
Section Two – Invest
    Chapter 4 – Stocks, Bonds and CDs
    Chapter 5 – Mutual Funds
    Chapter 6 – Exchange Traded Funds (ETFs)
Section Three – Safeguard Your Assets
    Chapter 7 – Life Insurance
    Chapter 8 – Property Insurance
    Chapter 9 – Investment Insurance

COVID-19 Impact

The COVID 19 Pandemic of 2020 has provided many excellent examples of why the chapters in Part I (saving, investing and safeguarding assets) are so important. With over 25 million Americans unemployed at one point, it was the highest percentage of unemployment since The Great Depression of the 1930's. Two major federal laws were passed just one year apart to provide much needed assistance to those Americans who faced severe financial hardship.

The Coronavirus Aid, Relief, and Economic Security (CARES) Act was passed in March 2020 to provide immediate financial assistance to tens of millions of Americans, many without any emergency savings. At an estimated cost of $2 trillion dollars, The CARES Act provided:

- Direct payments of up to $1,200 per single individual and $2,400 to married couples
- $500 per eligible child
- An additional $600 per week in unemployment benefits for four months

People with retirement accounts at least had a source of funds to access and the CARES Act encouraged withdrawals by waiving tax penalties for taking up to $100,000 from retirement plans. As reported in the July 2020 issue of Financial Advisor Magazine: "According to a May 2020 survey by YouGov on behalf of Bankrate.com, 14% of American with retirement savings, both those working and unemployed, have already tapped into those funds during the pandemic to meet their daily living expenses."

In March 2021, just one year after the passage of the CARES Act, The American Rescue Plan became law and offered additional federal support to individuals, small businesses, schools and state and local governments adversely impacted by COVID-19. Projected to cost $1.9 trillion, provisions of The American Rescue Plan to benefit individuals included:

- Direct payments of $1,400 to single Americans making less than $75,000 per year
- Payments of $2,800 to married taxpayers earning less than $150,000 per year
- Tax credits to reduce childhood poverty
- Increased funding to make health care coverage more affordable

Part I of How To Grow, Employ and Transfer (GET) Wealth not only explains ways to grow your assets by saving and investing, but also discusses how to safeguard your assets by making sure you have adequate insurance. Whether you are just starting to build wealth, are trying to reload savings accounts tapped due to COVID-19 or are looking for ways to continue building your assets, the information in Part I will help you speed up your financial growth to be better prepared for future economic disruptions.

Section One: Save

Chapter 1 – Emergency Savings Account (ESA)

*"Do not save what is left after spending
but spend what is left after saving."*
Warren Buffett

SAVE

Section One on how to GROW wealth describes great opportunities to SAVE using: 1) Emergency Savings Accounts (ESAs); 2) Tax-favored assets; and 3) Retirement plans and accounts.

CHAPTER PREVIEW

Establishing an Emergency Savings Account (ESA) is the first step you should take when starting a savings plan. Having a simple Emergency Savings Account does not sound like a big deal except that so few Americans have one.

As the COVID 19 pandemic of 2020 shut down huge numbers of businesses in the United States, lines of cars of people seeking help at food banks stretched for over a mile in some U.S. cities. Many people said this is the first time they had ever needed assistance to provide food for their families.

Millions of Americans lacked emergency funds to cover basic needs like food and rent which is why Congress quickly passed The CARES Act of 2020 to provide cash payments of $1,200 to 30 million U.S. residents. Just one year later, The American Rescue Plan Act of 2021 continued to provide cash assistance to millions of Americans who were unemployed and had suffered financial hardship due to COVID-19 business shutdowns.

The COVID-19 pandemic of 2020 was unique, but emergencies are not. Besides COVID-19, in 2020 Americans suffered from floods, wildfires, hurricanes and other natural disasters. You need to be prepared for financial emergencies so you are not counting on government help which might never come.

In this chapter, the following topics concerning saving will be discussed:
- Open an Emergency Savings Account (ESA)
- Needs vs wants
- USA Swiss bank account

1. OPEN AN EMERGENCY SAVINGS ACCOUNT (ESA)

If you do not already have an Emergency Savings Account (ESA), you are not alone. The Federal Reserve Board in May 2020 reported: "Nearly 3 in 10 adults were either unable to pay their monthly bills or were one modest financial setback away from failing to pay monthly bills in full. Sixteen percent of adults did not expect to pay all of their bills in full in the month of the survey in October 2019." An additional 12 percent said they were able to cover their current bills but could not do so if they had a $400 unexpected expense on top of their current bills. This survey was done before the massive layoffs from COVID-19.

Before opening an ESA, ask your employer if they can automatically withdraw funds from your paycheck and transfer those funds to a savings account. Employers who will transfer funds to their employee's accounts sometimes limit the financial institutions they work with. If they do not require that you have your ESA at a particular firm, look for a financial institution which offers no-fee or very low fee savings accounts with no or low minimum balance requirements. Since credit unions are nonprofit, they tend to be more willing to accept low balance savings accounts. Some credit unions only require a $5 initial deposit to open a savings account.

You have to become a member of a credit union to be able to use their services. Check to see who is eligible to join the credit unions you might be interested in joining. Membership requirements to belong to a credit union have been greatly reduced in recent years but still exist. Do not exclude banks from your search for an ESA but realize that big banks frequently want big clients, and you are not there – yet.

If your employer can automatically make direct deposits into your savings account, start having $10, $20 or $30 (or whatever you can afford) withdrawn from your paycheck and direct deposited into your ESA. Small regular deposits may not seem like much, but you will be surprised how they add up over time.

EXAMPLE 1: Bill makes very good money as a loan officer for a large mortgage company when times are good. During the Great Recession of 2008, Bill was laid off for several months. Bill did not have adequate savings to supplement the unemployment income he received and lost his house in foreclosure. He rented a small apartment until he was called back to work. Having gone through financial turmoil in 2009, once back to work, Bill set up an ESA at a local credit union, funded by a deposit of $50 every paycheck that his employer withdrew and forwarded to his ESA. When COVID-19 hit and Bill was again temporarily laid off, Bill had funds available in an ESA to supplement his unemployment checks and continued making his mortgage payments.

How much you are putting away is far less important than getting into the habit of saving money on a regular basis. Set a goal for your ESA to have three to six months of living expenses available to you for emergencies. When starting out, make your financial goals reasonable. Do not get discouraged if you temporarily have to reduce your regular deposits to cover unforeseen expenses. Just keep saving something.

2. NEEDS VS WANTS

> *"Too many people spend money they earned to buy things*
> *that they don't want to impress people they don't like."*
> *Will Rogers*

What are you willing to give up in order to be financially secure? Many people claim they cannot afford to save because they are living paycheck to paycheck. But several of these same people eat out frequently, lease new cars every three years and pay five dollars for a cup of coffee every morning that they could make at home for 50 cents.

EXAMPLE 2: Sarah hates to cook. Her stove and microwave are so clean from lack of use that she has to dust them once a month. On those rare occasions when Sarah does not eat out, she has food delivered and sometimes pays more for the service fee and tip than for the food. Sarah claims she "needs" to eat out when this is clearly a "want."

How often have you gone to a restaurant and ordered multiple glasses of wine that could be purchased at Costco or Wally's Wine World for under $20.00 a bottle. Usually, you can get four glasses per bottle. Instead of constantly going out to eat, Sarah decides to invite her friends over for dinner with each person bringing a bottle of the favorite wine and hopes her friends will return the invite so they can collectively save money.

Going out to eat should be a special occasion, not a requirement. If you do not know how to cook or hate to cook, there are numerous companies that will deliver prepared foods to your door. If you hate to eat alone, invite the food delivery person to join you for dinner.

Until you have decent balance in your ESA, keep your car an extra year beyond your normal holding period to save money. Or scale down your vacation plans. If you are worried about what your friends might think about you trying to save money, remember that friends do not let friends get into debt that could be avoided with a financial plan that funds an Emergency Savings Account.

3. USA SWISS BANK ACCOUNT

Treat your ESA like a secret Swiss bank account off in a scenic distant haven. Leave it untouched until absolutely necessary. Although withdrawals from your ESA should be penalty free, remember that the E in ESA stands for Emergency. If you think that you can easily tap into your Emergency Savings Account, you will. It defeats the purpose of having an ESA if you decide your desire for a triple shot of caffeine from a drive-by café is a critical need every morning.

EXAMPLE 3: Sue has set up an ESA at the bank where she has a checking account. She knows that her ESA is intended to cover emergencies, but she feels she has a great opportunity to join three of her friends who are traveling to St. Kitts. Sue will be saving so much by sharing costs with her friends that she decides she cannot afford not to go. Sue withdraws $1,000 from her ESA and promises herself that she will again start saving (seriously this time) once she returns from her trip.

Mentally place your ESA inside a safe deposit box at a Swiss bank. Your ESA should be available when you need it but tightly restrict how you classify a need.

CHAPTER SUMMARY

You need to have a savings account to cover unexpected expenses. It is virtually impossible to be financially secure if you have a stack of unpaid bills that are accumulating high finance charges. Establish an ESA at a financial institution that charges minimum fees and make regular deposits, no matter how small, to the account. Save the ESA for true emergencies, otherwise it is an ATM.

TAKE ACTION

- Set up an Emergency Savings Account at a credit union or bank which offers no fee accounts and has low minimum balance requirements.
- Authorize automatic deposits (however small) to be made to your ESA on a regular basis. Gradually increase your deposits if and when your income goes up.

- Review your ESA statements once a year when preparing your taxes. Check your progress yearly while you again remind yourself that this is an emergency only account.

Chapter 2 – Tax-Favored Assets

*"In the long run, it's not just how much money you
make that will determine your future prosperity.
It's how much of that money you put to work
by saving it and investing it."*
Peter Lynch

CHAPTER PREVIEW

*Utilizing tax-favored investments is a second way to GROW your
savings. Certain types of investments are taxed less, taxed later or not
taxed at all. Logically, the more money you keep after paying taxes,
the more your wealth will grow.*

To encourage people to save, Congress has passed several laws
providing tax benefits to savers, including the recent SECURE Act of
2019. While several tax breaks like unlimited property tax deductions
and home equity loan deductions for individual taxpayers have
recently been reduced or eliminated, tax incentives to save have
increased.

In this chapter, the following tax-favored assets will be discussed:
- Tax-reduced investments
- Tax-free investments
- Tax-deferred investments

1. TAX-REDUCED INVESTMENTS

To encourage people to save, Congress has passed laws which
provide more favorable tax treatment for certain types of income.
Qualified dividends and capital gains provide income that is taxed at
a lower rate than your wages and interest from accounts at banks and
credit unions. For savings that are not in an IRA or retirement account,
consider building a portfolio of investments which pay qualified

dividends and capital gains to increase what you keep by sending less to the tax collectors.

Qualified Dividends

Qualified dividends are paid by most companies that are based in the U.S. Qualified dividends can also be paid by foreign companies if their stock is traded on U.S. exchanges, the company is incorporated in a U.S. possession, or they benefit from a comprehensive tax treaty with the U.S.

Income which is not considered to be from qualified dividends includes interest from bank and credit union accounts, real estate investment trust (REIT) dividends, money market mutual fund dividends and special one-time dividends. Ordinary dividends are taxed at higher income tax rates.

To understand how qualified dividends, increase your ability to save, you need to know your current tax bracket. The U.S. income tax tables for individuals are shown below in Tables A, B and C. Here are the individual federal tax rates for 2021 which determine your tax bracket:

Table A: Single taxpayers

Taxable Income	Tax Rate
$0 to $9,950	10%
$9,951 to $40,525	12%
$40,526 to $86,375	22%
$86,376 to $164,925	24%
$164,926 to $209,425	32%
$209,426 to $523,600	35%
Over $523,600	37%

Table B: Married filing jointly

Taxable Income	Tax Rate
$0 to $19,900	10%
$19,901 to $81,050	12%
$81,051 to $172,750	22%
$172,751 to $329,850	24%
$329,851 to $418,850	32%
$418,851 to $628,350	35%
Over $628,350	37%

Table C: Heads of Households

Taxable Income	Tax Rate
$0 to $14,200	10%
$14,201 to $54,200	12%
$54,201 to $86,350	22%
$86,351 to $164,900	24%
$164,901 to $209,400	32%
$209,401 to $523,600	35%
Over $523,600	37%

To determine your tax bracket, start with the appropriate Table (A: single taxpayers; B: Married filing jointly; and C: Heads of Households). Go to the range showing your taxable income. Taxable income is the number you report on your tax return which is after deductions are taken out. Check your last tax return to determine your taxable income. Once you find the range where your taxable income falls, the percentage on that line is your tax rate and therefore your tax bracket.

EXAMPLE 1: Christine and Donald are married and together earn taxable income (after deductions) of $95,000 per year. According to Table B above, they are in the 22% tax bracket because their $95,000 taxable income falls between $81,051 and $172,250. For every additional dollar of ordinary income that Christine and Donald earn, they will send our friends at the IRS 22 cents ($1 minus 22%).

Now that you know how to determine your tax bracket, use Table D below to compare your tax rate for ordinary income with the lower tax rate for qualified dividends and capital gains.

Table D: Qualified dividends and capital gains

Unmarried taxpayers		Married filing jointly	
Taxable income	Tax rate	Taxable income	Tax rate
$0 - $40,400	0%	$0 - $80,800	0%
$40,401 - $445,850	15%	$80,801 - $501,600	15%
Over $445,850	20%	Over $501,600	20%

Table D (above) shows that lower income individuals (which includes many retirees) might pay no income taxes (as in zero) on their qualified dividends and capital gains. Higher income taxpayers also benefit since their top rate for qualified dividends and capital gains is 20% vs a top tax rate of 37% for ordinary dividends and interest from bank and credit union accounts.

EXAMPLE 2: Michael is unmarried and earns taxable income of $87,000. According to Table A above, Michael is in the 24% tax bracket (taxable income between $86,376 and $164,925). Michael earns $1,000 of qualified dividends from investments. From Table D above, although Michael is in the 24% tax bracket for his ordinary income (his salary and bank interest), the $1,000 of qualified dividends he received from his investment account is taxed at 15% instead of 24%.

Qualified dividends can be extremely beneficial for retirees relying on income from their investments to supplement Social Security and withdrawals from retirement plans and accounts.

EXAMPLE 3: Judy and Sam are retired and together earn $65,000 per year of ordinary taxable income. According to Table B, their taxable income of between $19,901 and $81,050 puts them in the 12% tax bracket. Judy and Sam also earn $4,000 of qualified dividends. Table B shows that they will pay no taxes on the $4,000 of income from qualified dividends since their taxable income is under $80,800.

Capital Gains

Capital gains are the profits you receive from the sale of assets that you have owned for at least 12 months. The gains might be from the sale of investments that have gone up in value or from mutual funds that sold appreciated securities in the last year. Capital gains might also be earned from the sale at a profit of real estate other than your primary residence. The first $250,000 of gains from the sale of your house could be tax-free. Double the $250,000 for married couples selling their home.

Congress has provided substantial income tax incentives to buy and hold certain assets like stocks, mutual funds, ETFs and real estate. If you own these assets for at least 12 months, Table B shows that you could pay less tax when those assets are sold.

EXAMPLE 4: Fred bought 100 shares of Microsoft for $150 per share. Two years later, Fred sells the 100 shares for $180 per share. Since the price per share of Microsoft increased by $30 over the two years that he owned the shares, Fred has a taxable gain of $3,000 (100 shares times $30 a share = $3,000). Because Fred held the shares for over 12 months, he qualifies for capital gains treatment. Fred is single and has taxable income of $90,000. He is in the 24% tax bracket for ordinary income. According to Table B, above, the $3,000 of capital gains will be taxed at 15% instead of 24%.

The sale of real estate other than your primary residence could also generate capital gains.

EXAMPLE 5: Linda and Ken bought a vacation house for $100,000 ten years ago. They sell the house for $150,000 and have a capital gain of $50,000 (Sale price of $150,000 minus the purchase price of $100,000 = a gain of $50,000). Together, Linda and Ken have taxable income of $90,000 so they are in the 22% tax bracket (taxable income between $81,051 and $172,750). Since they owned their vacation house for more than 12 months, they qualify for capital gain treatment on the $50,000 gain. According to Table D above, the $50,000 of capital gains will be taxed at 15% instead of their ordinary tax rate of

22% (taxable income of up to $80,000 for a married couple results in a 12% capital gains rate).

2. TAX-FREE INVESTMENTS

Even better than paying lower taxes with tax-favored assets is paying no income taxes. While it always sounds good to be able to invest and not pay taxes on gains, tax-free investments could have restrictions on how the gains are used or even being able to access these investments based on your income. Roth IRAs, education savings accounts and municipal bonds are some of the tax-free investments we discuss below.

Roth IRAs

Traditional IRAs are tax deferred. To encourage people to invest in IRAs, in exchange for being able to deduct the amount you put into a Traditional IRA, the income taxes are postponed until a later date. The theory is to get a tax deduction when you are working and are in a high tax bracket and take the funds out of an IRA when you are retired and in a lower tax bracket and send the IRS less.

Roth IRAs provide no up-front tax deduction, so you are investing money that has already been taxed. Instead of any gains being tax-deferred like in a Traditional IRA, gains withdrawn from a Roth IRA are income tax-free. This is a huge benefit for people who anticipate being in a high tax bracket later in life because they have a substantial amount of tax-deferred savings or because they plan to continue to work after age 70.

EXAMPLE 6: Linda is a well-paid senior manager at a large corporation. She has consistently invested in the 401(k) plan at work, so she anticipates being in the 24% tax bracket in retirement. Because she already has substantial tax-deferred income coming from her 401(k), Linda invests in a Roth IRA outside of work. Unlike deposits to her 401(k), she does not receive a tax-deduction but the gains in her Roth IRA are tax-free rather than tax-deferred. When combined with her potentially taxable Social Security (Chapter 16) and taxable

401(k) withdrawals, withdrawals from Linda's Roth IRA will provide additional funds without increasing her tax liability.

Not everyone can contribute to a Roth IRA. Single taxpayers earning over $140,000 in 2021 cannot contribute to a Roth IRA. Between $125,00 and $140,000 of income, contributions to a Roth IRA are reduced for single taxpayers. Married taxpayers who file jointly cannot contribute to a Roth IRA if their income in 2021 is over $208,000. Their Roth IRA contributions are reduced if they earn between $198,000 and $208,000. While Congress provides tax incentives to encourage people to save, they restrict those taxpayers most likely able to save from participating in a Roth IRA. Strange logic.

Education Savings Plans

To encourage people to save for college expenses, Congress has authorized Section 529 plans and Coverdell Accounts. Gains from these accounts are tax-free if used to pay for qualified education expenses not only for college students but for K-12 education as well. To reduce the likelihood, you will have to take out huge student loans to pay for college, investing early can pay great dividends with small regular deposits.

After-tax money is deposited into these accounts. Unlike pre-tax contributions to retirement plans which are taxed as they are withdrawn, there is no up-front tax benefit to investing in 529 plans, except for a state income tax deduction that is offered by some state programs.

The benefit to these plans is that any gains in the accounts are federal income tax-free if the funds are used for qualified education expenses. Due to a recent change in the federal income tax laws, 529 funds can now be used to pay for private K-12 expenses as well as college and post-graduate programs.

Since 529 plans are run by the states, each plan can have different provisions and tax treatment can vary. Gains in 529 accounts that are not used for qualified educational expenses may be subject to income tax penalties. Please consult with your state 529 administrators and your tax advisor regarding information about a particular plan.

EXAMPLE 7: Mary and Ken are a married couple with three children who they hope will all attend college. Before each of their children reached their first birthday, Mary and Ken established 529 accounts for them. Not only did they contribute regularly to each account, but they asked family members who wanted to give gifts to their kids to instead contribute to their 529 accounts.

According to the Investment Company Institute (ici.org), there were $329 billion of assets in all Section 529 plans as of the end of June 2018. Savings plans held $304.1 billion and prepaid tuition plans held the remaining $24. 8 billion.

Municipal Bonds

Governmental entities like states, counties, cities, public schools, etc. borrow huge amounts of money to construct government buildings, roads and operate schools. These loans are frequently structured as municipal bonds. As with most loans, the borrower (the governmental entity) needs to pay interest on the loan to the lender (bond buyer).

To reduce the cost to taxpayers who are usually ultimately responsible to pay back these loans/bonds, Congress permits the interest to be federally income tax-free. Depending on the state, a municipal bond might also be exempt from state income taxation. This is done to encourage residents to purchase their local bonds.

EXAMPLE 8: The Hooterville Community School District wanted to build a new high school. Once mostly farmland, Hooterville has grown rapidly since a new manufacturing plant was constructed two miles from Downtown Hooterville. Since they lacked the funds to build the new school, the citizens of Hooterville approved the sale of $25 million of municipal bonds to investors. The money from the sale of the bonds was used to construct the new school. Property taxes will pay back the $25 million borrowed by issuing the bonds plus interest on the bonds. Since Hooterville is a governmental unit, the interest received by investors who bought the school bonds is federally tax-free.

While municipal bonds are usually tax-free, not every taxpayer will benefit to the same degree by investing in municipal bonds. The interest rate paid on municipal bonds is usually lower than the rate paid on similar maturity taxable bonds. Therefore, municipal bonds are best purchased by taxpayers in higher tax brackets (22% and above).

EXAMPLE 9: Heather is a single business owner who earns taxable income of $215,000 placing her in the 35% tax bracket. She receives $1,000 per year of tax-free income so she keeps all $1,000. Heather also receives $1,000 of taxable income from her credit union savings account and since she is in the 35% tax bracket, she sends 35% ($350) of her taxable income to the IRS. Heather is willing to accept a lower interest rate on income from tax-exempt municipal bonds as long as she winds up with more than she would have with higher-paying taxable income after sending the taxes owed to the IRS.

The lower your tax rate, the less you send to the IRS. If you are not in one of the three highest tax brackets (32%, 35% or 37%), it is unlikely you benefit from investing in municipal bonds, regardless of what your friendly bond hawking salesperson tells you.

EXAMPLE 10: Bill is a retired single individual with taxable income of $34,000 per year and therefore is in the 12% tax bracket. Bill has $25,000 invested in a CD paying him 2% at a bank so he receives $500 per year of taxable income. Bill not surprisingly dislikes paying income taxes, so he is considering purchasing $25,000 of shares in a mutual fund investing only in municipal bonds which pays 1% tax-free per year. While Bill would keep 100% of the 1% tax-free income he would receive, he would not come out ahead taxwise. Since Bill is in the 12% tax bracket, he sends $60 (12%) of the $500 to the IRS and keeps $440 ($500 minus $60 for taxes equals $440). If Bill receives 1% tax-free on $25,000 invested in the mutual fund, he will receive only $250. Obviously, $440 after-tax is better than $250 tax-free.

To determine if a tax-free interest rate is better for you than a taxable rate, subtract your income tax rate from 100. This is the percent you keep after you pay taxes If you are in the 35% tax bracket, 100 minus 35 equals 65. If you are considering investing in a taxable bond paying 2.0% per year, multiply 2.0% by 65 and your return after taxes is 1.3%. A bond paying 1.5% tax-free is therefore a better investment than a taxable bond paying the higher 2.0% but will be reduced by 35%.

Using the same investments, a person in the 12% tax bracket keeps 88% (100 minus 12 equals 88). Multiply the taxable bond paying 2.0% by the retention rate of 88% and you keep 1.8%. The same municipal bond paying 1.5% tax-free is therefore not a good deal (1.5% vs 1.8% after tax) for a person in a lower tax bracket since they send relatively little (in this case 12%) to the IRS.

While most municipal bonds provide a great benefit in the form of federal tax-free income, they are riskier than U.S government obligations. Cities, states, school districts and other local governmental entities rely on property and sales tax revenue to pay the interest due and to be able to redeem their bonds. If local governmental revenues are down due to a recession, municipalities might default on their bonds. Knowing the financial strength of the governmental entity issuing a municipal bond and the rating before the bond matures is important information that investors and bond holders need to monitor.

You can obtain municipal bonds by purchasing individual bonds (Chapter 4), investing in bond mutual funds (Chapter 5) and through exchange traded funds (Chapter 6) that contain municipal bonds.

3. TAX DEFERRED INVESTMENTS

"Compound interest is the eighth wonder of the world.
He who understands it earns it, he that doesn't pays it."
Albert Einstein

Unlike tax-free investments (general obligation municipal bonds) which are not taxed, accounts which are tax-deferred means taxes are delayed, not eliminated. The benefits come from postponing paying taxes until when you anticipate being in a lower tax bracket (Table A, B and C above), so you send less to the IRS. The most common situation is where you are in a lower tax bracket once you have retired.

Tax-deferred investments like retirement plans and accounts provide unique opportunities to save because gains in these plans and accounts are allowed to compound on a tax-deferred basis. If you are in the 22% tax bracket, you send the IRS annually 22% of the interest you earn in a savings account other than an IRA at a credit union or bank. Inside a tax-sheltered retirement plan or account, none of that interest or gain is taxed until it is withdrawn. That 22% that would have gone to the IRS every year is allowed to compound without being taxed until taken out of the account. The additional gains from tax-deferred compounding add up significantly if left untouched for several years.

The vast majority of tax-deferred investments are held in accounts primarily intended to provide retirement income. Because retirement plans and accounts are such an excellent way to save, these investments will be discussed in greater detail in upcoming Chapter 3.

With most retirement plans and accounts, you receive a tax deduction for the funds you contribute to your tax-deferred account which could lower your tax bracket. When you are retired, assuming you are then in a lower tax bracket, you will pay less income taxes on those "pre-tax" contributions when they are withdrawn from your tax-deferred account.

While people focus on the immediate tax-deduction they receive by investing in retirement accounts, the benefits of tax-deferral can be far greater. Delaying taxation until you are in a lower tax bracket and being able to grow your account without an annual tax bite has a lot more potential value. This is why we will be spending so much time discussing tax-deferred savings options available to you in upcoming Chapter 3.

Defined Contribution Retirement Plans

Older pension programs were defined benefit plans. As the name implies, a defined benefit amount was promised to workers when they retired. The amount usually was determined by a formula which took in account the number of years you worked for the company and how much you were paid.

Defined benefit plans have been largely replaced by defined contribution plans. Again, as the name implies, workers contribute a portion of their wages to the defined contribution plan but do not get a specific defined benefit in return once they retire.

EXAMPLE 11: Heather is a 35-year-old married college professor who has $500 per month ($4,800 per year) deducted from her paychecks and deposited into the 403(b)-retirement plan administered by the college. Heather's taxable income will be lowered by $4,800 since she elected to contribute that amount into her 403(b)-plan account. The $4,800 will hopefully grow inside the 403(b) account on a tax-deferred basis so no taxes are owed until the money is withdrawn from the plan. After Heather retires, her income tax bracket drops from 22% to 12%. As she withdraws funds from her retirement account, she sends 12% to the IRS instead of 22% which was her tax rate while she was working.

If you work for a large company which offers a retirement plan, you probably are probably participating in a defined contribution plan like a 401(k), 403 (b), 457 or IRA SIMPLE. All of these retirement plans will be discussed in greater detail in the next chapter.

On the other hand, funds in a defined contribution plan can be transferred to a new employer's plan, an IRA or spent by the employee/account owner. You have far more control over your retirement funds in a defined contribution plan which is especially important if you change jobs.

Individual Retirement Accounts (IRAs)

If you do not have access to a retirement plan where you work, set up your own retirement plan with an individual retirement account

(IRA) which is discussed in greater detail in Chapter 3. Basically, IRAs frequently enable you to reduce taxes on earned income while saving for the future in a tax-deferred account. You control how the funds are invested based on how much risk you are willing to accept.

Tax-Deferred Annuities

Some investors want to set aside additional funds for their retirement above and beyond what they have invested in their retirement plan at work or in their IRA. Annuities can provide the sheltered tax-deferred compounding but do not offer the immediate tax deduction that motivates people to invest in retirement plans and IRAs.

Tax-deferred annuities are issued by insurance companies. Annuities are given special tax treatment so that you do not pay income taxes on gains until the gains are withdrawn. While some annuities are placed inside IRAs so that all the withdrawals are taxable, most annuities are "non-qualified" which means the investor did not receive a tax deduction up front. Only the gains are taxable.

EXAMPLE 12: John is a single taxpayer who did not participate in his employer's 401(k) plans because he changed jobs frequently and does not want to commit to funding a retirement plan with any one company. When John decided to take funding his retirement seriously, John contributed the maximum allowed to his 401(k) plan. John wants to have additional money compounding on a tax-deferred basis, so he invests after-tax funds in a tax-deferred annuity. Although John will not receive a tax-deduction for deposits made into his annuity, he will get the benefit of tax-deferred compounding.

Life insurance policies also have the potential to provide tax-deferred income since the cash value in universal life and whole life policies grows without being taxed until withdrawn other than by borrowing or when paid as a tax-free death benefit. Life insurance is discussed in Chapter 7.

CHAPTER SUMMARY

Tax-favored investments included qualified dividends and capital gains. You pay less income tax if your investments generate qualified dividends. Capitals gains are assets held for at least one year and are taxed at the same low rate as qualified dividends. Tax-deferred investments postpone income taxes to a future date. Traditional IRAs are a common tax-deferred investment along with tax-deferred annuities. Tax-free investments are primarily municipal bonds issued by states, cities and other government entities. The interest from municipal bonds is wholly or partially tax-free to reduce the interest expense paid the governmental unit issuing the bonds.

TAKE ACTION

- Purchase investments which pay qualified dividends to reduce your tax burden. If you are a conservative investor, consider investments in large companies that are less volatile.
- If you have minor children or grandchildren, contribute to a 529 education account for their college expenses.
- Invest in a Roth IRA or in the Roth portion of your company retirement plan if you believe that you will be in a mid to high tax bracket in retirement.

Chapter 3 – Retirement Plans and Accounts

"The question isn't at what age I want to retire,
it's at what income."
George Foreman

CHAPTER PREVIEW

Retirement plans and accounts provide a third and probably best opportunity for you to save and GROW wealth because of the generous tax incentives provided by Congress to encourage people to save. Most recently, the SECURE Act of 2019 increased incentives to save.

Think about your future. When you are no longer able to work, how will you pay for your living expenses? Social Security was never intended to be the sole source of income for retirees, and it is very likely that benefits will be less generous in the future. Social Security is discussed later in Chapter 16.

While COVID-19 may have set back your plans to save for retirement, the American economy will recover. No matter how small your contribution might be, start or maintain the habit of paying yourself first by investing for what is likely the many years when you are retired.

CARES Act of 2020

Under normal circumstances, you should not tap into your retirement accounts before you are retired. But the negative economic impact of COVID-19 was anything but normal when 25 million Americans became unemployed within two months. For many, their retirement accounts have become the emergency savings accounts discussed in Chapter 1.

In March 2020, the Cares Act became law in response to the devastating impact of COVID-19 on the economy. In addition to providing direct payments to families and enhanced unemployment benefits, The CARES Act changed several regulations that gave people easier access to their retirement accounts. The idea was that unemployed individuals needed access to their retirement funds now, without the early withdrawal penalties intended to keep you from tapping into your funds prematurely.

According to The Wall Street Journal of 6/5/2020: "The U.S has allowed those affected by the coronavirus and economic downturn to take up to $100,000 out of retirement savings accounts, either individual retirement accounts or employment linked 401(k)-type plans, without an early withdrawal penalty. It has allowed them to borrow up to another $100,000 from 401(k) plans."

Retirement accounts have become an emergency fund for workers who are suddenly unemployed with no other source of income. Although tapping into your retirement accounts should never be taken lightly, COVID-19 further demonstrated the value of saving. The combination of having an Emergency Savings Account (ESA) and funds saved for retirement are what will give you financial security.

Start Small But Start

Many people hope to retire in their mid-60's while they are still healthy and active to be able to enjoy their retirement. But before you retire, realize that the average life expectancy of Americans is currently 79 years. If you retire at 62, on average, you could be living without a paycheck for 25 or more years. How do you plan to cover 25 plus years of expenses if you lack adequate savings?

According to Financial Advisor Magazine: "A recent Federal Reserve report showed a substantial number of Americans have no retirement savings. Thirteen percent of those who are over 60 years of age and 17% of the 45-to-59 age group have no financial cushion. Twenty-six percent of those ages 30 to 44 have no retirement savings, and 42% of the 18-to-29-year-old group have not started saving." (9/2019)

In this chapter, three types of retirement plans and accounts will be discussed:

- Employer sponsored retirement plans
- Individual retirement plans
- Tax-deferred annuities

1. EMPLOYER SPONSORED RETIREMENT PLANS

Congress views employer sponsored retirement plans as the most efficient way to encourage people to save for retirement and has provided substantial tax benefits to participate in these plans. You do not get many tax breaks and to GET wealth, you need to take advantage of the few you qualify for.

The SECURE Act of 2019 increased incentives to save for retirement while the CARES Act of 2020 provided people with much easier access to their retirement accounts due to the economic hardship caused by COVID-19.

Two major categories of employer-sponsored retirement funds are defined benefit plans and defined contribution plans. While defined benefit plans have been largely replaced by defined contribution plans, it is important to understand how they are different.

Defined Benefit Plans

The older style pension plans that were common in the 1950's are defined benefit plans. These plans define how much of a benefit you should receive in retirement, usually based on your wages and how long you were with the company or government unit (cities, counties, states, etc.). The company or governmental body assumes the risk of making sure there are sufficient funds in the plan to pay for the benefits they promised. Defined benefit plans are now far less popular than defined contribution plans because companies and governmental bodies do not want the liability to run them.

Unfortunately, many defined benefit plans are "underfunded" which means they have less money in the plan than actuaries' project will be needed. For example, the State of Illinois currently has a projected underfunding of $50 billion. Not a typo. Promises have been made to Illinois teachers, police officers, firefighters, etc. to pay "defined" retirement benefits but sufficient funds have not been set aside to cover these obligations. Illinois is not alone. The total estimated amount of unfunded pension liabilities by states is approximately five trillion dollars according to the American Legislature Exchange Council in 2020.

Who is going to cover these obligations when the money runs out? Should taxpayers bail out companies that paid excessive bonuses to executives while ignoring the contractual obligations they made to their lesser paid employees? Stay tuned.

Defined Contributions Plans

Defined contribution plans are now more common. As opposed to your employer assuming the risk to make sure there are sufficient funds to pay the benefits they promised, in a defined contribution the employee/plan participant assumes the investment risks and rewards.

This is both good and bad. Unlike a defined benefit plan, your defined contribution plan funds move with you if and when you leave your employer. Since the old 30 years and out at one company is also out, the flexibility of a defined benefit plan is huge.

There are several types of retirement plans that employers can offer their staff. Employer sponsored plans are extremely popular because they can be easily funded by payroll deductions. Workers can put regular payments into their accounts and get a tax-deduction for what they are saving. Funds in retirement plans grow on a tax-deferred basis which means they will be taxed when taken out of the plan. The goal should be to get a tax deduction when you are working and take the funds out when you are retired and will probably be in a lower tax bracket.

Employers prefer defined contribution plans since they are not required to make sure that there are sufficient funds in the retirement plan to cover the defined benefits that were promised to workers.

Some of the more common employer sponsored defined contribution retirement plans are:

401(k)
403(b)
457
SIMPLE
SEP
401(k) Plans

The most popular type of employer sponsored plan is the 401(k). Approximately four trillion dollars are invested in 401(k) plans.

While many companies offer 401(k) plans because they have discontinued their defined benefit plans, 401(k) plans offer some unique benefits that are not available in traditional pension programs. 401(k) plans offer 1) Tax –deferral; 2) Availability of investment options; and 3) Transferability of assets.

In a 401(k) plan, employees agree to have a portion of their salary, hourly wages, bonuses, etc. taken out of their paycheck and deposited into a savings account. Tax-deferral occurs because the withdrawals are made before the compensation is received by the employee. First, you get to deduct the compensation you deposit into your savings account, so you do not pay income taxes on the money you have put aside, Second, any growth (market gains or dividends earned) on the money in your 401(k) account are not taxed until you take the funds out so even greater compounding takes place.

Besides the huge tax breaks provided by tax-deferral, 401(k) plan assets can be moved from one retirement plan to another without triggering income taxes. This is extremely important because you may want to retain control of your retirement funds and not leave them behind with your former employer.

In 2021, employees can contribute a maximum of $19,500 per year pre-tax. Individuals who at least 50 years old can contribute up to an additional $6,500 per year to their account.

Solo 401(k) Plans

What happens if you have never worked at or have left a for profit company that offers a 401(k) plan, but you want access to a retirement plan with 401(k)-type features?

Self-employed individuals might be able to establish their own "solo" 401(k) as long as the business has one owner and only one employee is the owner's spouse. Both the owner and the owner's spouse, if employed by the company, can contribute to the solo 401(k).

Solo 401(k) plans are ideal for self-employed individuals who want the flexibility of contributing to a retirement plan when times are good but no longer work for a large company.

EXAMPLE 1: Aaron is an engineer who takes a buyout offer from his employer and in order to work as a contract engineer. Aaron sets up a consulting company as a limited liability company (LLC) where he is the sole owner. Aaron also establishes a solo 401(k) in the name of his new LLC and requests a custodian-to-custodian transfer of his 401(k) balance from his former employer's plan to his new retirement plan. Since the transfer was handled directly from one 401(k) plan to another, Aaron continues the tax-deferral without incurring any income tax liability. Similar to his former 401(k) plan at his former employer, in 2021, Aaron can contribute the lesser of 100% of his compensation to his solo 401(k) or $19,500 per year ($25,000 if he is at least 50 years old). Some solo 401(k) plans allow participants to borrow from their plan like those at large companies.

Since you are not required to contribute to your solo 401(k) every year, these small plans are especially attractive to self-employed individuals like real estate agents who alternate between having great years where they desperately need to reduce their taxable income and very slow years where they cannot afford to contribute to their plans.

In 2021, employees can contribute a maximum of $19,500 per year pre-tax. Individuals who are at least 50 years old can contribute up to an additional $6,500 per year to their account.

403(b) Plans

Non-profit organizations like public colleges and universities, not for profit hospitals, charities, etc. offer 403(b) plans that closely resemble the 401(k) plans at most for profit companies. Like 401(k) plans, employee contributions are pre-tax so deposits to the plan are taxed when taken out, hopefully when an employee has retired and is in a lower tax bracket.

In 2021, employees can contribute a maximum of $19,500 per year on a pre-tax basis to their account. Employees who are at least 50 years old can contribute up to an additional $6,500 per year.

457 Plans

Employees of state and local governments along with certain tax-exempt IRC 501 (c) organizations frequently have access to 457(b) plans which operate similar to 401(k)'s or 403(b)s.

Higher level employees at select government and non-government entities sometimes are able to participate in 457(f) plans. These programs are limited to management, so they are beyond the scope of this book.

In 2021, employees can contribute a maximum of $19,500 per year to their account on a pre-tax basis. Individuals who are at least 50 years old can contribute up to an additional $6,500 per year.

SIMPLE Plans

A SIMPLE Plan is just that – simple. Unlike 401(k) plans which can be complex to administer and therefore expensive to maintain, some SIMPLE plans only charge $10 per participant per year.

In exchange for less administrative costs, employers are required to contribute yearly according to one of the following formulas: 1) A dollar for dollar match of up to 3% of compensation which only involves those participating in the plan; 2) A contribution equal to 2% of compensation to all eligible employees, including those not contributing to the plan; or 3) A contribution of at least 1% of compensation in at least 2 out of 5 years to permit employers having financial difficulties to temporarily reduce their HR expenses.

SIMPLE Plans do not allow participants to borrow from their plan accounts. This discourages some individuals from participating since frequently loans from 401(k) plans is an important feature many want.

In 2021, employees can contribute a maximum of $13,500 per year pre-tax to a SIMPLE plan. Individuals who are at least 50 years old can contribute up to an additional $3,000 per year to their account.

EXAMPLE 3: George is 60 years old and the owner of a small company. George wants a retirement plan that he can participate in along with his employees who want to contribute. He wants to avoid the high administrative costs of a 401(k) plan, so George establishes a SIMPLE plan. Three of his employees decide to participate so George decides to match up to 3% of the employees' compensation that is put into the plan. The administrative cost is only $10 per participant. George contributes the maximum of $13,500 per year plus the $3,000 extra since he is over 50 years old. Although George pays an additional $4,000 for the match (a large portion going to himself as the highest plan contributor), the tax deduction he receives is substantial. By offering a retirement plan to his employees, he is increasing the likelihood they will stay with his company.

SEP Plans

Employees cannot contribute to SEPs unlike more popular retirement programs like 401(k)s, 403(b)s, SIMPLE plans. In a SEP, the employer can contribute the lesser of 25% of compensation or $56,000.

Because all contributions are made by the employer, SEP plans are frequently used by smaller privately held companies where the owners are actively involved in the operation.

In 2021, employers can contribute up to the lesser of 25% of an employee's eligible compensation up to a maximum of $56,000 per year.

3. INDIVIDUAL RETIREMENT ACCOUNTS

Not all employers offer retirement plans to their staff. People can still save for retirement by contributing to either traditional IRAs or Roth IRAs. Depending on their income and if their spouse has access to a retirement plan.

Traditional IRAs

The attractiveness of a traditional IRA is that you get a tax deduction when you contribute, the funds hopefully grow on a tax-deferred basis and then are taxed at a lower rate when you withdraw the funds when retired.

In 2021, eligible individuals can contribute up to $6,000 per year to a traditional IRA. Individuals who are at least 50 years old can contribute up to an additional $1,000 per year to their account.

Contributions to a traditional IRA might reduce your income taxes. Whether or not you can claim a tax deduction depends on your income and if your spouse is eligible to participate in their employer's retirement plan. See Table A and B below.

Table A

If you are not covered by a retirement plan at work, the following rules apply for 2021:

Filing Status	Modified AGI 2021	2021 Deductibility
Single or head of household or qualifying widower	Any amount	Full deduction up to the contribution limit
Married filing jointly or separately with a spouse who is not covered by a plan at work	Any amount	Full deduction up to the contribution limit

Married filing jointly with a spouse who is covered by a plan at work	$198,000 or less	Full deduction up to the contribution limit
	Over $198,000 but less than $208,000	Partial deduction
	$208,000 or more	No deduction
Married filing separately with a spouse who is covered by a plan at work	Less than $10,000	Partial deduction
	$10,000 or more	No deduction

Table B

If you are single and covered by a retirement plan at work or if you are married and one spouse is covered by a retirement plan, the following rules apply for 2021:

Filing Status	Modified AGI 2021	2021 Deductibility
Single or head of household	$66,000 or less	Full deduction
Single or head of household	$66,001 - $75,999	Partial deduction
Single or head of household	$76,000 or more	No deduction
Married filing jointly or qualifying widow (er)	$105,000 or less	Full deduction
Married filing jointly or qualifying widow (er)	$105,001 - $124,999	Partial deduction
Married filing jointly or qualifying widow (er)	$125,000 or more	No deduction
Married filing separately	Less than $10,000	Partial deduction
Married filing separately	$10,000 or more	No deduction

Roth IRAs

A major difference between Roth IRAs and traditional IRAs is that Roth IRAs grow tax-free, and traditional IRAs grow tax deferred. But the tax-free growth from a Roth IRA comes at a cost.

When funds are taken out of a traditional IRA, they are taxed as ordinary income because individuals received a tax deduction when the money was deposited into the IRA.

In 2021, eligible individuals can contribute up to $6,000 per year to a Roth IRA. Individuals who are at least 50 years old can contribute up to an additional $1,000 per year to their account.

Table C

If you are not covered by a retirement plan at work (a spouse or married partner could be covered).

Single, head of household, or married filing separately, and you did not live with your spouse at any time during the year	$121,999 or less	Full contribution
Single, head of household, or married filing separately, and you did not live with your spouse at any time during the year	$122,000 - $136,999	Partial contribution
Single, head of household, or married filing separately, and you did not live with your spouse at any time during the year	$137,000 or more	Not eligible
Married filing jointly or qualifying widow (er)	$192,999 or less	Full contribution
Married filing jointly or qualifying widow (er)	$193,000 - $202,999	Partial contribution
Married filing jointly or qualifying widow (er)	$203,000 or more	Not eligible

Married filing separately	Less than $10,000	Reduced amount
Married filing separately	$10,000 or more	Not eligible

3. TAX-DEFERRED ANNUITIES

Annuities are investments offered by insurance companies. While annuities do not have the backing of the FDIC (for banks) or the NCUSIF (for credit unions), fixed annuities are backed by the assets of the insurance company which issued the annuity. The assets in variable annuities are kept separate from the assets of the insurance company offering the annuity.

Annuities are tax-deferred which means that income taxes will eventually have to be paid on the gains when they are withdrawn from the annuity. This feature can provide huge benefits for individuals who might otherwise have to pay taxes every year on their gains and reduce the amount that is compounding. Over time, tax-deferred compounding can produce significantly higher returns than investments which are not under some type of tax-sheltered umbrella.

Tax-deferred annuities can be an excellent retirement account for individuals who do not have access to an employer-sponsored retirement plan and have maxed out or do not qualify to contribute to an IRA. Annuities held outside of an IRA or retirement plan are non-qualified which means the investor does not receive a tax deduction for funds placed in the annuity. The tax-deferred compounding still provides an important benefit even without the up-front tax deduction.

Although it is possible to purchase annuities that have low fees, most annuities are sold by licensed agents who are compensated by fees built into the annuities. The insurance companies which pay the salespeople a commission to place their annuities will impose a surrender charge if the annuity buyer does not hold the policy long enough for the insurance company to recoup the commission they paid. If you are considering buying an annuity, be sure to ask not only about annual fees you would be paying but also how long you need to own the annuity before it can be moved without getting hit with a surrender charge.

Fixed Rate Annuities

Annuities which offer investors a specific interest rate are fixed income products. They look similar to CDs from banks and credit unions but without the FDIC or NCUSIF insurance. Fixed income annuities are instead backed by the assets of the issuing insurance company which can be very substantial. Always check the ratings for the strength of an insurance company before purchasing an annuity. Ratings are discussed in Chapter 7.

EXAMPLE 3: John is a 70-year-old retiree who needs income to supplement his Social Security payment and is more concerned about losing money than growing his assets. John purchases an annuity that pays a fixed rate of three percent per year for a five-year period. Since he has the interest deposited monthly directly into his bank account, income taxes are owed on the amount he receives every year. At the end of the five-year period, the principal John invested can be withdrawn without a penalty.

Fixed rate annuities frequently pay a higher rate of interest than CDs with the same maturity dates. Annuities are not as secure as federally insured CDs but if backed by a financially strong insurance company, they are worth looking at if the interest paid is substantially better than CDs of similar length.

Indexed Annuities

Investors seeking to have some participation in financial markets but with less downside risk should consider indexed annuities. Investors can select to receive gains based on the performance of an index like the S & P 500. Unlike a mutual fund based on the S & P 500 which will fluctuate in value, indexed annuities participate in the upside of the markets but preserve your principal if the index declines. In exchange for limiting downside movement, indexed annuities will cap the amount investors can receive.

EXAMPLE 4: Mary would like to participate in the stock markets but lost money in the 2008 downturn and now wants to safeguard her principal. Her insurance agent sells Mary an indexed annuity which offers to pay 75% (participation rate) of what the S & P 500 returns over a 12-month period subject to a maximum of five percent (5%) per year (cap rate). If the S & P 500 goes up, Mary could enjoy a return that beats the fixed rate annuities. If the S & P 500 drops over 12 months, the value of Mary's account does not decline.

While index annuities do provide better returns in positive performing markets, they are not good investments if the participation rate and cap rates are low.

Variable Annuities

Variable annuities (VAs) give individuals the opportunity to invest in stock and bond funds while offering tax-deferral since they are housed in an annuity. The investment choices in a variable annuity are far more extensive than indexed annuities and fixed rate annuities. VAs also frequently offer benefits that lock in gains at certain intervals, have guaranteed income rates and enhanced death benefits. Nothing is free in life or perhaps in death (to be determined) and you have to decide when purchasing a variable annuity if the extra fees for extra benefits are worth the cost.

Insurance companies keep the assets in variable annuities separate from company assets. If the insurance company went bankrupt, assets in their variable annuities would not be exposed to bankruptcy claims. Traditional fixed rate annuities and indexed annuities are subject to the claims paying ability of the company.

EXAMPLE 5: Mary is a single lady who recently received an inheritance from her mother. Mary is working at a company that does not offer a retirement plan so she contributes the maximum she can to an IRA. She wants to set aside some of the money she inherited in an investment which will hopefully supplement her income once she retires in about 10 years. Mary invests in a variable annuity and places her funds in moderately aggressive funds. When Mary retires, she instructs the insurance company to make monthly payments into her bank account based on the value of her VA. She will receive income from the annuity for the rest of her life with any undistributed funds going to her nieces and nephews.

Variable annuities are more complicated investments than fixed rate annuities because they offer many investment choices and multiple payout options. Although the fees in a VA are higher than some other investments, they might be worth the cost if they provide benefits, you value and that you cannot obtain elsewhere. Make sure whoever is offering to sell you the variable annuity takes the time to explain the pros and cons not only of the VA but of each feature for which you are paying for.

CHAPTER SUMMARY

Saving by participating in retirement plans and accounts is one of the most effective ways to grow wealth. There are many tax benefits that come with saving for retirement through either an employer sponsored plan or an individual retirement account (IRA). Once you have maxed out the tax benefits available through retirement plans and IRAs, consider investing after-tax funds in tax-deferred annuities.

TAKE ACTION

- Contribute to the retirement plan available through your employer unless you have concerns that the plan is not being properly administered.
- Invest in an individual retirement account (IRA) if you do not have access to an employer sponsored retirement plan, are seeking to rollover your retirement funds to a traditional IRA to continue the tax-deferral or you are able and willing to fund a Roth IRA.
- Purchase tax-deferred annuities if you do not have access to an employer sponsored retirement plan or you have maxed out your ability to contribute to a retirement plan or IRA and you want to put away additional funds for retirement. Tax-deferred annuities can also be used as an investment option in rollover IRAs.

Section Two: Invest

Chapter 4 – Stocks, Bonds and CDs

"If you aren't willing to own a stock for ten years, don't even think about owning it for ten minutes. Put together a portfolio of companies whose aggregate earnings march upward over the years, and so, also will the portfolio's market value."
Warren Buffett

INVEST

Section Two on how to GROW wealth discusses options to INVEST like: 1) Stocks, bonds and CDs; 2) Mutual funds; and 3) Exchange traded funds (ETFs).

In just a few weeks, COVID-19 quickly destroyed years of gains in the U.S. stock markets. According to an article in the 4/20/2020 issue of Bloomberg Businessweek: "The S&P 500 may have set a new low for this episode on March 23, barely a month after its last record high, on Feb. 19. That's unheard of in the history of bear markets since 1929. It took on average 373 trading days from record high to bottom during those 10 declines ..."

COVID 19 was a wake-up call for investors to realize that stock and bond markets can be volatile. The more you understand about your investments, the more likely you will make better decisions about the types of investments that are most suitable for you to own as you work to grow your wealth.

The Rule of 72

Before we discuss saving and investing, you need to accept the fact that it is virtually impossible to double your money in one week while investing for retirement. Sorry. Investments can possibly double with time, but you have to be patient and apply formulas that show it can be accomplished.

The odd list price of this book is $10.72, purposely to remind you of The Rule of 72. Far more fortunes are made over time as opposed to overnight.

The Rule of 72 states that if your investments earn 10% per year, you will double your money in 7.2 years. Conversely, if you earn 7.2% per year, you will double your money in 10 years.

Especially with your long-term retirement accounts, apply the Rule of 72. First, learn the past rate of return of your investments. Then divide the number 72 by the past rate of return. The result is the number of years it would have taken to double your money in that particular investment option.

EXAMPLE 1: You own an ETF that has a published rate of return of 8%. Divide 72 (The Rule Number) by 8 (the 8% projected return) and it equals 9 (the number of years). Therefore, it will take you 9 years to double your money if your rate of return is 8%.

EXAMPLE 2: Assume you made a one-time investment six years ago in a mutual fund which has a stated rate of return of 12% per year for the past six years. If you divide 72 (The Rule Number) by 12 (the average annual rate of return for the past six years) it equals 6 (the number of years). You can therefore double your money in six years at 12% percent per year.

Your odds of growing your wealth will improve if you research potential investments before you buy and then give compounding time to work its magic. Again, remember The Rule of 72: You will double your money in 10 years if you average 7.2% per year or double in 7.2 years if you average 10% per year. Look for steady growth, not one-hit wonders.

CHAPTER PREVIEW

Stocks, bonds and CDs are the first group of items we will discuss as possible investment options.

If you are participating in a 401(k) or 403(b) plan at work, you are probably investing in mutual funds. Since you are hopefully making regular deposits into your retirement plan, mutual funds are an excellent way to invest those contributions because shares of a mutual fund can be purchased in pieces or fractions equal to the amount you are investing.

While mutual funds are the most common investment options for retirement plan deposits, many people prefer to hold individual issues of stocks and bonds when they are investing outside of a retirement plan. People excited about investing in stocks usually know what Amazon does, what Apple makes or what Disney movie is attracting a record number of viewers. It is admittedly difficult to get excited about owning a mutual fund even though the fund might own Amazon, Apple and Disney.

There is nothing wrong with buying individual stocks or bonds. Just remember that mutual funds and exchange traded funds (EFTs) are diversified, and individual issues are not. You need more time to research and more money to invest in order to construct a diversified portfolio that could be easily obtained by investing in a mutual fund or ETF both of which are covered in upcoming chapters.

In this chapter, the following investment options will be discussed:
- Individual stocks
- Individual bonds
- Certificates of Deposit (CDs)

1. INDIVIDUAL STOCKS

When people talk about buying "stock" they are usually discussing purchasing shares of a corporation that is owned by shareholders. A privately held company is owned by one or more people who hold all the shares of the company. Ownership of a privately held company is restricted so the shares are not bought and sold to the general public.

Owning individual shares of stock can be both good and bad. If you guess correctly and buy a stock that goes up substantially in value, you will gain the envy and admiration of those investors who bought a "cannot lose" stock like dog.com shortly before it went bankrupt. Timing is important. A share of Amazon cost $18 per share when it first went public in May 1997. As of July 30, 2021, the price per share of Amazon was over $3,000.

Before you invest in anything, research what you are considering buying. Publicly traded companies are required to provide massive amounts of information to the public. Since the information can be difficult to understand, several companies will offer recommendations on what stocks to buy and sell. Some services are free in the hope you will move up to a paid service from the same company. Other services are available for a subscription fee. Be aware that no service, no matter what they claim, can predict how financial markets and individual stocks will move with 100% accuracy. If someone could foretell the future, the Mega Lotto would be won by the same person every week.

EXAMPLE 1: Fred only buys Apple iPhones and decides to buy stock in Apple which is a publicly traded corporation. Assume shares of Apple stock are selling for $100 per share when Fred decides to buy 50 shares. At $100 per share, it will cost Fred $5,000 ($100 times 50 shares equals $5,000) plus possible trading fees. Two years later, if Apple shares are then selling for $200 per share, Fred's shares are now worth $10,000. Fred decides to hold onto his 50 shares even though he realizes that Apple could face additional competition in the future that might cause the share price to drop from $200 per share.

In addition to the price of the stock, you might have to pay a transaction fee to purchase the stock. Some brokerage firms will waive fees in order to get you to open an account. Again, there is no free lunch served at the Brokerage Bar B-Q. Investment firms are not charities. What you do not pay in transaction fees you might instead compensate the company by receiving little or no interest on the amount you keep in the money market fund within your account. Look for fees. Like weeds in your lawn, they are there.

Since diversifying your investments is extremely important, if you do not have enough money to invest in at least five companies, then you should stay away for individual issues of stock and instead invest in mutual funds (next up in Chapter 5) or in ETFs -Exchange Traded Funds (coming soon in Chapter 6).

2. INDIVIDUAL BONDS

Like owning individual stocks, it is possible to own individual issues of bonds. Buying a bond is similar to lending money to someone. When you purchase a bond, the corporation or government institution accepts your money and agrees to pay you interest until the bond (loan) is paid off. The interest from bonds can be taxable or tax-free.

Taxable Bonds

The U. S. government is the largest issuer of bonds. When you read that another multi-trillion-dollar government program has been approved, the way the money is raised to fund the program is by issuing bonds. The U.S. government is borrowing money from investors and agrees to pay the investors interest until they repay the loan (bond). When there is a gap between the tax revenue coming and government spending, that results in a deficit that is covered by more borrowing.

As reported in The Wall Street Journal of 8/13/2020: "The federal deficit more than tripled in the first 10 months of the fiscal year, as government spending to combat the coronavirus continued to outpace federal tax collection, the Treasury Department said Wednesday. The U.S. budget gap totaled $2.8 trillion from October through July, $224 billion more than the $867 billion gap during the same period a year earlier."

In addition to bonds issued by the U.S. government, you can also purchase taxable corporate bonds. Companies issue bonds to raise capital to finance construction of new plants which are later closed, cover operating expenses and most importantly, to pay obscene compensation to corporate executives.

EXAMPLE 2: You want to have fixed income payments in retirement, and you are not looking for the investment to grow in value. You decide to purchase a corporate bond issued by Apple which matures on May 1, 2040. The bond has a coupon of 2.0% and you purchase $20,000 at face value (par value). As with most bonds, this bond pays interest twice a year, on May 1 and six months later on November 1. Since the coupon is 2% and you own $20,000 at face value, you will earn $400 per year ($20,000 times 2% equals $400). On May 1 and November 1, the investor will receive $200 (one-half of $400).

Tax-Free Municipal Bonds

Governmental units like states, counties, cities and school districts frequently need to borrow money for long term projects like constructing schools, building bridges or replacing water and sewer lines.

Why would someone buy a bond approved by the Hooterville School Board instead of buying a corporate bond issued by Apple? The simple answer is that the school bond pays tax-free interest while the corporate bond pays interest that is taxed.

Instead of borrowing funds for projects from financial institutions, government units will issue municipal bonds to raise money. Unlike the interest paid on corporate bonds which is taxable to investors, municipal bond interest is usually tax-free. This is permitted by the IRS to reduce the interest rate the government unit has to pay.

Individuals in higher tax brackets (discussed in upcoming Chapter 10) like the tax-free income. Even though the bonds pay less interest than a corporate bond, investors pay little or no income tax on the interest and therefore earn a better "after tax" rate of return than if they got a higher taxable rate and then had to pay a portion of the interest received to the IRS or to their state tax agency.

EXAMPLE 4: Charlie is a very successful business owner who is currently in the highest federal income tax bracket (37%) and lives in a state that has a five percent income tax. Charlie has an effective tax rate of 42% (37% to the IRS plus 5% to his State equals 42%). Charlie decides to invest in a 10-year school bond paying 2% tax free instead of a 10-year corporate bond paying 3%. He keeps all of the 2% tax-free income but would send 42% of the 3% taxable interest to the IRS and his state tax authority which would leave him an after-tax rate of 1.75% (100 minus 42% equals 58% times 3% equals 1.75%).

Although receiving tax-free income is attractive to individuals in higher tax brackets, you need to evaluate the financial security of the governmental entities issuing the bonds before you buy. Unlike U.S. Treasury obligations, state and local governments cannot print more money to cover deficits. The Wall Street Journal of 8/15/2020 reported: "As of July 31, there were a total of 50 municipal defaults, according to Municipal Markets Analytics -the most since 2011."

COVID-19 has put a spotlight on the finances of U.S. cities and states. With unemployment at near record levels, general revenues from taxes are projected to drop which will impact the ability of some governmental entities to make bond payments. Leave low quality junk bonds where they belong in an economic recession – in the junkpile.

Inflation and Higher Rates

One additional consideration that you need to address when buying bonds is the impact of inflation on fixed income investments. The historical average rate of inflation is 3.22% so realize that if inflation begins to climb, the earnings power of the income from your bond will drop.

If interest rates increase, the value of your bond will decline. This could happen given the massive amounts of Treasury obligations that are being issued to finance the deficit. but if the U.S. government continues to borrow to cover deficits,

3. CERTIFICATES OF DEPOSIT (CDs)

A certificate of deposit (CD) is similar to an individual bond. CDs issued by banks or credit unions usually are backed by either the FDIC (Federal Deposit Insurance Corporation) for banks and the NCIC (National Credit Union Association) for credit unions.

Although some CDs pay a variable rate of interest, most certificates of deposit pay a fixed rate.

Traditional Certificates of Deposit (CDs)

For conservative investors who are extremely worried that they are going to lose money and are less concerned about how much they earn on their money, CDs are a great fit. You invest in a CD for a particular time period. Think of it as lending the bank your money and they pay you a fee called interest.

The financial institution now takes your money and tries to find people who will borrow your money from them at a higher rate than they are paying you. If the bank is paying you one percent on your CD, they may try to lend it out as a car loan earning them four percent. The difference between what they pay you and what someone pays them is the spread. The bigger the spread, the more profitable the bank.

Although low interest rates have reduced the appeal of CDs, they are still attractive to conservative investors who want the comfort of knowing that they will get their principal back on the maturity date.

EXAMPLE 5: Bill is 75 years old and currently owns stocks, bonds and has a savings account paying a low rate of interest. Bill wants a certain portion of his investments to not fluctuate in value to cover future health care expenses. He withdraws some of the funds from his savings account to construct a "ladder" of insured CDs at a credit union where he is a member. Bill invests $10,000 in a CD maturing in one year paying 1.0% per year. He invests an additional $10,000 in a CD maturing in two years paying 1.25% and he invests $10,000 in a three-year CD paying 1.5% per year. Bill will receive a higher rate of interest from the CDs than if he had left the funds in a savings account because he gave up penalty-free access to his funds. But by laddering the maturities, Bill is no more than 12 months from a maturing CD. When the one-year CD matures, Bill can either cash out the CD without a penalty or invest in a three-year CD since he now has CDs maturing in 12 months and two years.

Hybrid CDs

As with ice cream, plain vanilla CDs were just not exciting enough for many investors. Investment bankers created hybrid CDs to attract investors wanting to participate in the stock market without risking their principal.

EXAMPLE 6: Bill wants a CD with FDIC backing but dislikes the low interest rate being paid on CDs. He purchases a hybrid CD with FDIC backing if the CD is held to maturity in five years. The interest is paid annually on the anniversary date and is based on the performance of a group of five stocks: Apple, Duke Power, General Motors, JP Morgan Chase and Target. If all five stocks go up in value (even slightly) over a specific 12-month period, the investor gets an eight percent coupon. If one or more of the stocks drops in value over the 12 months, the investor receives a money market rate of .25% (one-quarter of one percent).

CHAPTER SUMMARY

Individual stocks and bonds can be good investments for people willing to do research about the company issuing the stock or the issuer of a bond. Unless you have a lot of money to invest, it is difficult to construct a diversified investment portfolio buying individual stock issues.

Certificates of deposit (CDs) are usually issued by banks and credit unions and are usually insured by the FDIC (banks) or the NCUA (credit unions)

TAKE ACTION

- Research a company whose product you use and recommend to others. See what analysts who follow the company say about their prospects. If you like what the analysts have to say, buy however many shares of stock in the company that you can afford to hold for a year.
- Purchase U.S. government bonds if you are subject to high state taxes since income from U.S. Treasury obligations are state tax

free. Buy corporate bonds if the issuing company is profitable and the interest rate is adequately higher to compensate you for state taxes and the higher risk of not having the backing of the U.S. government.

- Stagger the maturity dates of your CDs so that they mature approximately 12 months from another CD. When the term of a CD ends, purchase another CD that matures 12 months from another maturity.

Chapter 5 – Mutual Funds

"Investing should be more like watching paint dry
or watching grass grow. If you want excitement,
take $800 and go to Las Vegas."
Paul Samuelson

CHAPTER PREVIEW

Mutual funds are a second type of investment you can use to GROW wealth.

Mutual funds are pools of stocks and/or bonds that are bought and sold by a team of portfolio managers for a fee. Mutual funds are a popular investment choice for people who want to own stocks and/or bonds but are unable or unwilling to put together a portfolio of individual issues.

Mutual funds provide investment diversification since multiple individual issues are usually held in a fund. It is the role of the portfolio managers to select investments which they believe will perform well. Good performance attracts and retains investors. Poor performance by fund managers usually results in potential investors not investing in the fund or selling their shares in the fund and investing elsewhere.

In this chapter, the following types and features of mutual funds will be discussed:
- Stock and bond funds
- Target date funds
- Mutual fund share classes

1. STOCK AND BOND FUNDS

If you decide to own stocks, would you rather own large amounts of a few stocks or small amounts of several stocks? Obviously, if you were fortunate enough to buy stocks like Amazon or Microsoft at $50 per share several years ago, then holding a few companies is the right call.

Instead of buying one share of Amazon for over $2,000, consider investing $2,000 in a mutual fund that has Amazon in their portfolio along with shares of stock of several other companies. If the price of Amazon stock goes up along with the price of other stocks in the mutual fund, then you will do well over time.

EXAMPLE 1: Heather wants to save for her retirement, but she works at a small company that does not offer their employees a 401(k) or similar type of plan. Heather decides to open a Traditional IRA and authorizes $60 each month to be electronically transferred from her credit union to her IRA. Of the $60 automatically sent to her IRA, $30 is to be deposited into a mutual fund investing in the stock of very large companies. The mutual fund is classified as large growth with average risk by a rating company. The other $30 being invested monthly is deposited into a mutual fund investing in small companies. This mutual fund is designated as small growth with above average risk.

As opposed to owning a diversified mutual fund with many different stocks, you might have greater returns if your portfolio only held excellent stocks and no losers. We wish it was that easy.

Compare investing to sports. The last professional baseball player with a season-ending batting average over .400 was Ted Williams in 1941. He finished the year at .406 to be precise. That phenomenal batting average means that Ted Williams got a hit only 4 out of every 10 times (40%) when he came to bat that year. He failed sixty percent (60%) of the time to get a hit.

If someone has only picked stocks that have always gone up in value, they have been extremely quiet about that incredible accomplishment. If true, every person seeking wealth would invest with that person and pay handsomely for the opportunity. Selecting winning stocks is part skill (research), timing (having funds to invest) and luck (authorizing a purchase before the stock heads upward).

Back to baseball. For many decades, Babe Ruth held the record not only for the most home runs but also for the most strikeouts. Investing to hit only home runs might produce a few real winners but you will also fail plenty of times. For many people, the safer way to invest is to select mutual funds or exchange traded funds (Chapter 6) and hold them for longer periods of time.

2. TARGET DATE FUNDS

Many people investing in their employer's retirement plan (401(k), 403 (b), etc.) wind up using target date mutual funds. They are currently the most popular option in retirement plans.

A target date fund is designed to have the fund portfolio become more conservative as a client gets closer to retirement. The theory is that when you are several years away from retirement, you can afford to be more aggressive with your investments. If you are a younger investor and you encounter a bad market which causes your portfolio to drop substantially, you have time on your side to wait until the markets hopefully correct.

An individual who is close to retirement, does not have that same time element on their side. As a person gets closer to the target age on the fund, the portfolio managers move more funds into bonds and less into stocks. Although not always true, fixed income investments like bonds are historically (but not always) less volatile than stocks.

EXAMPLE 2: Bill is currently 40 years old and plans to retire in 25 years. He does not feel comfortable selecting various investments and just wants to put his retirement account on auto pilot looked after by professional money managers. Bill decides to invest in the mutual fund offered through his employer's plan that has a target date 25 years from now. Bill contributes to the same target date fund but the composition of investments in that fund gradually become more conservative the closer he gets to the target date when he expects to retire.

A word of caution about target date funds. When you are close to retiring, it may not be a good time to be invested primarily in bonds if the stock markets are performing well. As your retirement nears, take advantage of unbiased financial advice that might be available to you as a participant in your employer-sponsored plan. Your retirement funds may need to support you for decades. A portfolio consisting mostly of bonds may not be adequately diversified to provide the growth you will need to cover future increases in the cost of health care, housing and living expenses.

3. MUTUAL FUND SHARE CLASSES

No-load mutual funds are purchased without a sales charge being imposed. A potential investor deals directly with the company that is managing the mutual fund portfolio. The mutual fund company hires customer service people to assist potential and current investors with the selection of mutual funds offered by that company.

A load mutual fund is usually purchased through an investment advisor. The mutual fund company pays the advisor to handle the sale of their products. The fees paid to the investment advisor depend on the share class of the mutual fund that is purchased. Some of the most common mutual fund share classes are A, B, C and R and are discussed below.

Class A Shares

Class A shares charge investors a fee at the time of purchase that comes out of the initial investment. Class A shares are considered a good option for people who are planning to hold the mutual fund for an extended period of time since the annual fees are lower after paying the initial sales charge.

EXAMPLE 3: John is retired and receives a substantial pension from his former employer where he was a plant manager. He hopes his two grandchildren aged 5 and 7 will attend college and John wants to help fund their education. Based on the recommendation of his investment advisor, John invests $10,000 in 529 plans for each of his grandchildren. To compensate his financial advisor for his research, John invests in Class A shares which pay his advisor a 4% fee. The $10,000 invested in Class A shares will be reduced by 4% to cover the advisor's fee so $9,600 is actually invested. Since Class A shares have a lower annual administration fee than other share classes, John feels he will recover the up-front fee over time.

Class B Shares

Class B shares have become less popular in recent years. Unlike Class A shares which reduce the value of the money being invested by the up-front sales charge, Class B shares invest 100% of the money into the shares of the mutual fund. Since the mutual fund company compensates financial advisors who recommend their Class B shares, the mutual fund company will impose a surrender charge if an investor withdraws money from the company before a certain number of years have passed. Class B shares have higher annual administrative fees than Class A shares, so regulators have determined that investments in Class B shares are not always in the best long-term interest of consumers.

EXAMPLE 4: Barb is 40 years old and wants to build a portfolio that she can tap into after she retires but earlier if she needs the funds. She contacts a financial advisor who recommends purchasing the Class B shares of a particular growth mutual fund. Barb invests $5,000 and all of her $5,000 is used to purchase Class B shares of the mutual fund. The investment advisor is paid 5% at the time of the purchase even though the fee does not initially reduce the value of her investment. While Barb pays no up-front sales charge, if she has to access the funds in the first 12 months, she will pay a surrender charge of 5%. The surrender charge drops to 4% after 12 months, 3% after two years, 2% after three years, 1% after four years and zero percent if she holds the investment for five years.

Class C Shares

Class C shares are somewhat like Class B shares since advisor compensation does not initially reduce the amount invested. Like Class B shares, there is a fee imposed if shares are not held for a certain period of time. The difference is that Class C shares only have to be held for one year before no back-end surrender fees are imposed while Class B shares have a holding period of five or more years. The compensation paid to advisors recommending Class C shares is usually 1% of the amount being invested. While obviously lower than the 4% or 5% compensation paid to advisors who recommend Class A and Class B shares, the 1% fee associated with Class C shares is paid every year, usually for 10 years.

If an investor knew with absolute certainty how long they were going to own a particular mutual fund, then it would be much easier to determine the most cost-effective share class to buy. Long-term investors would benefit from Class A shares and short-term investors might come out ahead with Class C shares even with their higher annual expense ratios. Understand the differences between the share classes before you buy a mutual fund and invest using your best estimate as to how long you are likely to own that particular fund.

EXAMPLE 5: Ann is 30 years old and just received an inheritance of $40,000. She currently rents an apartment but would eventually like to own a condo once she has a better idea where she might be employed for several years. Ann purchases the Class C shares of a growth and income mutual fund recommended by her financial advisor. Like Class B shares, 100% of the money she places in the mutual fund will be invested without a sales charge. Unlike the multi-year surrender charge schedule of Class B shares, after only 12 months, there will be no surrender charges. In exchange for a very short one-year surrender charge period, Class C shares impose a higher annual fee which could cost Ann more if she holds the fund for 10 or more years.

Class R Shares

Class R shares are exclusively for retirement plans like 401(k)'s or SIMPLE plans. Class R shares charge lower annual fees since it is anticipated that funds will be in the retirement accounts for extended periods of time. Logically, smaller fees enable the retirement accounts to grow more if less is taken out for administrative expenses. Access to lower fee share classes is another reason why saving though retirement plans and accounts is frequently a better option to grow your wealth.

EXAMPLE 6: Mary works at a large non-profit hospital which offers employees a 403(b) plan. Contributions to the retirement plan are invested in Class R shares which have lower fees because the 403(b) plan has thousands of participants. Mary enrolls in the hospital's 403(b) plan with the help of the HR department of the hospital, instead of employees or investment advisors paid by the mutual fund company.

Investing in Class R shares is a preferred way to contribute to a retirement plan. Assuming a mutual fund has the same portfolio and only the share classes differ, the lowest fee structure will result in better performance over time. The lower fees associated with Class R shares may reduce the amount of available administrative services a participant receives. But overall, Class R shares enable a participant to obtain better returns over time.

CHAPTER SUMMARY

Mutual funds are an excellent way to invest a specific amount of money in a diversified pool of stocks or bonds. Since mutual funds can be purchased in fractional shares, they are very well suited for retirement plans where employees are making automatic deposits to their accounts or where an investor wants to invest small amounts regularly.

TAKE ACTION

- If you want to invest in a mutual fund, decide if you are looking for growth, income or a combination of both. Should you prefer to do your own research, invest in no-load mutual funds and utilize the services provided by mutual fund companies. If you are not comfortable researching your options, then hire an investment advisor to provide you with recommendations on what mutual funds to purchase.
- Invest in target date funds in a 401(k) or 403(b) plan if you want an investment pool which becomes more conservative as you get closer to retirement. Younger individuals have time on their side to ride out bad markets. Target date funds automatically restructure the holdings to become more conservative as investors age and do not have the luxury of time to weather market upheavals.
- Make sure you completely understand what a mutual fund company is charging you for their services and how their representatives are being compensated. There are several mutual fund share classes including A, B, C and R. Each share class has a different fee structure which will impact your returns. If you have a choice, select the lowest fee option that still provides the support services you want

Chapter 6 – Exchange Traded Funds (ETFs)

*"We have three baskets for investing:
yes, no, and too tough to understand."*
Charlie Munger (Berkshire Hathaway)

CHAPTER PREVIEW

Exchange Traded Funds (ETFs) are a third possible option to use for investing to GROW wealth.

According to Blackrock Asset Management, one of the largest issuers of ETFs, "Exchange traded funds offer diversified, low-cost and tax-efficient access to the world's investment markets. ETFs are designed to track the performance of specified indexes, less fees."

Because of these features, over the past few years, substantially more money has been invested in exchange traded funds (ETFs) than in mutual funds. CNBC.com in a post on11/9/2019 stated: "U.S.-based exchange traded funds have racked up a record $4 trillion in assets under management this year, with 136 ETF providers offering 2,062 ETFs to investors, according to research firm ETFGI."

For many investors, ETFs are the largest category of investments in their portfolio due to their transparency and lower fees. Once you have core holdings in ETFs, you can add individual issues of stocks, bonds and CDs to compliment the ETFs that you own. Mutual funds are likely to also be part of your combined financial assets through an employer-sponsored retirement plan.

In this chapter, three aspects of exchange traded funds (ETFs) will be discussed:
- ETF features
- ETF benefits
- ETF choices

1. ETF FEATURES

Exchange traded funds (ETFs) offer diversified portfolios like mutual funds. But unlike mutual funds which are priced at the end of each trading day after stock and bond markets have closed, ETFs trade like stocks so you can buy and sell them while the stock market exchanges are open.

Exchange traded funds are computer generated portfolios. In many cases, ETFs may look like mutual funds but the cost of owning ETFs is usually substantially less than comparable mutual funds.

An exchange traded fund classified as large cap growth, could include stocks like Apple (AAPL), Microsoft (MSFT) and Amazon (AMZN). An ETF considered a utility ETF might have in their portfolio Duke Power (DUK), Florida Power and Light (FPL) and Consolidated Edison (CON).

EXAMPLE 1: Bill wants to invest in healthcare stocks but does not have enough money to build a diversified portfolio of individual issues. Bill decides to invest in a healthcare sector ETF which holds positions in United Health (insurance), Pfizer (drugs), Abbott Labs (medical testing equipment) and Striker (medical) equipment. Because the health care companies held in Bill's ETF are selected by a computer program, the annual fees for the ETF are less than a quarter of the fees charged by a managed health care mutual fund that Bill was considering buying.

While it is possible for active portfolio managers to outperform passive investments like ETFs, the recent trend has been that the performance of passive funds beats the total return of similar actively managed funds over selected periods of time. Even if you add the cost of utilizing an investment advisor to help you select ETFs, since the annual fee for ETFs is lower than similar mutual funds, you could still wind up with less administrative costs than investing in mutual funds. This is a major reason why ETFs have grown so rapidly over the past 20 years.

2. ETF BENEFITS

Exchange traded funds are attracting more money than mutual funds. Compared to most mutual funds, ETFs offer lower fees, greater transparency and better tax efficiency.

Lower Fees

ETFs usually have lower expenses than mutual funds. Most ETFs are based on computer models as opposed to being actively managed like mutual funds. According to The Motley Fool, "In 2016, the average expense ratio of index ETFs was just 0.23% compared with a 0.82% average expense ratio of actively managed mutual funds and a 0.27% expense ratio for index equity mutual funds according to the Investment Company Institute."

EXAMPLE 2: Eric works for a large international company. His job requires that he travels extensively so he is not interested in spending time researching investments. Eric hires an investment advisor who recommends exchange traded funds with expense ratios under .25 percent. The advisor charges a fee to monitor the ETFs in Eric's portfolio and recommend additions and deletions. After paying the advisor's fee, the cost of the ETF plus the fee is less than the cost of a mutual fund that Eric was considering.

Greater Transparency

It is relatively easy to know the primary holdings in an ETFs at any time. Search engines like Yahoo Finance, Google Money and Money.com are just a few of the sources where you can get current prices for ETFs. While ETFs trade while the markets are open, mutual funds only trade at the end of the day.

Mutual funds do not offer the same high level of transparency as ETFs. Mutual funds report the composition of their holdings every quarter. Since many mutual funds are actively managed, portfolio managers are reluctant to publicize their holdings for fear that their competitors will copy their best ideas. While this might be true for some managers, statistics indicate that the majority of professional money managers have under-performed passive investments like ETFs and index mutual funds for well over 30 years.

EXAMPLE 3: Sue is interested in purchasing a diversified pool of stocks of the companies whose products she buys faithfully like Apple and Disney and whose services she uses like Amazon and Netflix. Sue researches and finds a large cap growth EFT holding stocks of many of the companies she supports. Sue buys 100 shares of the growth ETF. Unlike mutual funds which can be purchased in fractional shares, ETFs are normally bought in full shares. After her purchase, Sue can easily check periodically what are the major holdings in the ETF she owns. This enables Sue to confirm that the ETF is still invested in companies she likes.

Better Tax Efficiency

Although ETFs like mutual funds are combinations of investments (stocks, bonds, etc.) ETFs trade more like individual issues of stock. Mutual funds potentially generate "phantom income" every year when they distribute capital gains.

While ETFs held outside a retirement account frequently generate dividends and interest which are taxed, unlike annual mutual fund distributions, capital gains in an ETF are not generated until the shares are sold. It is therefore possible to time when you want to generate capital gains with ETFs, perhaps when you are retired and in a lower tax bracket.

EXAMPLE 4: Bill is one of those rare individuals who hates paying income taxes. For that reason, Bill likes to hold onto his investments for at least a year to qualify for the lower tax rates imposed on long term capital gains. Since he does not like capital gain distributions that he has no control over, Bill invests in ETFs rather than mutual funds. After Bill is retired, he is in a lower tax bracket which enables him to take advantage of the tax-favored rates for capital gains and qualified dividends.

3. ETF CHOICES

Exchange traded funds are relatively new compared to mutual funds which have been available since the 1920's and currently hold over $19 trillion in assets. One of the first ETFs was introduced in March 1993 by State Street Global Investors and it tracked the S & P 500. Exchange traded funds have become so popular that Bank of America estimates that $5.3 trillion will be invested in EFTs before the end of 2020. Compared to mutual funds which have existed for 100 years, by 2030, Bank of America is projecting that assets in ETFs will hit $50 trillion. There must be good reasons for this explosive growth.

EXAMPLE 5: Tina has mutual funds in her 401(k) at work. She wants to invest additional funds in stock markets that she could access without an income tax penalty. She opens an investment account and purchases an ETF that concentrates its holdings in large company technology stocks such as Apple, Microsoft and Intel. Tina also invests in an ETF which holds companies which are smaller, have good growth prospects and are not limited to a particular industry like technology.

Several sources now track ETFs and many offer recommendations for a fee as to which exchange traded funds you should buy. Free sources of information on EFTs include Morningstar.com, Yahoo finance, Google money and other search engines. Be prepared for free services like Morningstar to try and get you to trade up to their premium service which changes a fee. There is obviously nothing wrong with paying a fee for information if you use the service. If you want more personal attention, consider hiring an investment advisor to find ETFs that might be suitable for you.

CHAPTER SUMMARY

Exchange Traded Funds (ETFs) are investment products constructed by computer programs and could provide a diversified investment option similar to mutual funds. Exchange Traded Funds offer greater transparency and lower administrative costs than many managed mutual funds and investment accounts and more tax efficiency than mutual funds. There are currently over 2000 different exchanged traded funds. They can be as basic as the S & P 500 or as narrowly focused as an ETF that tracks small cap companies in India.

TAKE ACTION

- Decide which investment categories (large cap growth, small cap value, etc.) and which sectors (utilities, technology, energy, etc.) you want in your portfolio.
- Research and select those ETFs which you feel offer the best combination of performance, reasonable fees and composition of their holdings.
- Review your portfolio at the end of each quarter to determine if the ETFs in your portfolio are performing well relative to other similar ETFs. Adjust your portfolio holdings as needed, not just for the sake of making changes.

Section Three: Safeguard Your Assets

Chapter 7 – Life Insurance

"Fun is like life insurance.
The older you get, the more it costs."
Kim Hubbard

SAFEGUARD YOUR ASSETS

Section Three on how to GROW wealth discusses ways to SAFEGUARD your assets using: 1) Life insurance; 2) Property insurance; and 3) Investment insurance. What is the point of saving and investing to grow wealth if you fail to safeguard your assets?

CHAPTER PREVIEW

Life insurance is the first product we will examine that you should consider buying to safeguard your assets.

Upcoming Chapter 15 discusses managing debt like mortgages, credit cards and student loans. But you have to have something to manage, like money to pay off your debts.

Other than funeral home directors and cemetery operators, few people like talking about death. But since every life eventually ends, we need to be prepared for when death occurs.

Life insurance is a unique product that shows up when you need it most. When you die, life insurance can provide funds to replace the income that you provided your family.

We are not trying to push you to buy life insurance. But if you have debts and your family depends on you to help pay those debts, then you need to explore options to enable your family to have the funds they need to cover those payments after you die. Life insurance is one option that can provide those needed funds after you die.

It is not enough to have life insurance. Having the right kind of life insurance can play an extremely important role in safeguarding your assets. Buying the wrong type of insurance policy might cause you to drop your insurance coverage because you cannot afford the premiums. Then not only are you without life insurance but you also wasted money paying premiums for a non-cancelled policy.

To help you evaluate the pros and cons of life insurance, in this chapter, the following aspects of life insurance will be discussed:

- The need for life insurance
- Types of life insurance
- How to buy life insurance

1. THE NEED FOR LIFE INSURANCE

Do you have a mortgage, credit card debt, college loans, etc.? If you died in a car accident tomorrow, would your family have adequate funds to either pay off your debts or have a source of income to continue to make payments on your debts until they are paid off?

Many people seeking an estate plan will frequently say: "If I were to die ..." Unfortunately, the question is when you are going to die, not if.

Hopefully, your death is many years in the future. But whenever it occurs, will your family be able to pay the bills that you now cover?

EXAMPLE 1: Sharon and John purchased a house by taking out a large mortgage. As a two-income family with three young children, Sharon and John were able to make the monthly mortgage payments without incurring any financial hardship. Sharon dies in a car accident. Being young and healthy, Sharon did not feel she needed life insurance. John now has to make the monthly mortgage payment on his one income and has very little savings to help him make those payments.

Life insurance is cheaper when you are young because the likelihood of death is small. According to The Center for Disease Control and Prevention (CDC), the average life expectancy actually dropped to 78.8 years in 2020 due to COVID-19. As you get older and have more health issues, life insurance becomes more expensive since life insurance companies are more likely to have to pay out a death benefit the longer you own the policy.

In addition to paying a lower cost for life insurance when you are young because your life expectancy is long, younger individuals usually have fewer major health issues and therefore are more likely to be approved for life insurance. When you are 70 years old and decide you need life insurance, will you have any health conditions that would make you uninsurable?

Insurance Company Financial Ratings

When evaluating life insurance policies, always check to see how the life insurance company is rated. An insurance company needs to be financially strong enough to pay the death benefits you paid for when the time comes.

The Insurance Information Institute (iii.org) states on their website: "Five independent agencies – A.M. Best, Fitch, Kroll Bond Rating Agency (KBRA), Moody's and Standard & Poor's – rate the financial strength of insurance companies. Each has their own rating scale, its own rating standards, its own population of rated companies, and its own distribution of companies."

The Institute, which claims to have over 60 major insurance companies as members, goes on to recommend: "The agencies disagree often enough so that you should consider a company's rating from two or more agencies before judging whether to buy or keep a policy from that company." The rating scale for A.M. Best is shown below in Exhibit A.

Exhibit A

Best's Financial Strength Rating Scale

Rating Categories	Rating Symbols	Rating Notches
Superior	A+	A++
Excellent	A	A-
Good	B+	B++
Fair	B	B-
Marginal	C+	C++
Weak	C	C-
Poor	D	-

EXAMPLE 2: Sam decides he needs life insurance to provide funds for his wife to pay off the mortgage on their house if he were to die while the mortgage is outstanding. Sam also wants to make sure his wife has money to cover the household expenses he now pays and plans to have funds available to his children to attend college if he dies within the next 20 years. Sam receives a quote to purchase a life insurance policy from a company rated "B" by A.M. Best, one of the rating agencies. He thinks a "B" rated company is pretty strong until he learns that the "B" rating by A.M. Best is a middle rating and is listed as "Fair." Sam instead purchases a policy from a company rated "A+" which costs him more but gives him greater peace of mind that the company will provide the death benefits after he dies.

Contact information for the above-mentioned ratings agencies can be found at: iii.org. Before you purchase an insurance policy that you might own for 20 plus years, take the time to check out if the insurance company is strong enough to be there when your family needs them to pay on the policy.

2. TYPES OF LIFE INSURANCE

Many people assume that all life insurance policies are the same. Individuals believe you send the insurance company regular payments and when you die, your family gets a large check. If only life and life insurance was that simple. In this Chapter we will focus on: 1) Term insurance, 2) Universal life insurance and 3) Whole life insurance.

As a general rule, term insurance is considered to be temporary insurance while both universal life and whole life are sometimes referred to as permanent policies. Term life is temporary because it is valid for a certain number of years only as long as you pay the premiums. Classifying universal life and whole life policies as permanent is misleading since universal life and whole life policies are "permanent" only as long as the policy premiums continue to be paid usually by the person who is insured, or as long as adequate funds are in the cash value account of the policy to cover the premiums.

Since a person cannot build any kind of surplus in a term life policy, it is compared to renting an apartment as opposed to buying a house where you can build equity. It is not really a fair comparison since if you stop paying rent you will be evicted. If you stop making your mortgage payments, your lender can foreclose on the property, regardless of how much equity (value) you have built up. The difference is with permanent insurance, you could borrow from the cash value (if any) in the contract to cover premiums whereas you cannot tap into the equity in your house unless the homeowner takes out a home equity loan.

Term Life Insurance

Term life insurance, as the name implies, provides coverage for a designated period of time. The term might be 15 years, 20 years or 30 years. The insurance policy is valid as long as you continue to pay the premiums. Once you stop paying (other than having died or became disabled in some policies) then the policy ends. There is no cash value or surplus pool of money being built up in a term life policy which can cover the premiums when they are not paid.

If you buy a 30-year term policy, that does not mean you are obligated to pay for the policy for the full 30-year term. You might have taken out the policy to cover your mortgage if you die before it is paid off and to provide for the college education of your children if you died prematurely. After say 20 years, if your house is paid off, your kids have graduated from college and you have substantial funds in retirement accounts, you might decide you no longer need the term life policy so stop paying the premiums. Your coverage from the 30-year term policy will end but so do the payments.

Before you stop paying on your term life policy, consider your health situation. Do you have health issues that would prevent you from getting a new affordable life insurance policy? A major benefit of buying a 30-year term life policy when you are young and healthy is that the premium is fixed for the entire 30-year term. Even if you later become uninsurable, the policy cannot be cancelled as long as the premiums continue to be paid.

Term life insurance is usually best suited for younger married individuals who want to provide for their family in the event they die with financial obligations like an outstanding house mortgage and future college expenses for their minor children as well as the critical loss of the insured's income.

EXAMPLE 3: Justin is 40 years old, married with three minor children. Although his employer provides a $50,000 life insurance policy as an employee benefit to all their employees, Justin wants additional funds to be available when he dies to help his family cover living expenses, the outstanding mortgage on their house and pay for college for his three minor children. Since Justin is young, he decides that term insurance is his best option. Justin goes on-line and purchases a 20-year, term life policy with a $250,000 death benefit for only $500 per year. If Justin were to wait until he turns 50 to purchase a 20-year, term life policy with a $250,000 death benefit, that same policy (assuming he qualifies health-wise) would cost $700 per year.

Although most life insurance agents can sell term insurance policies, the commission they receive does not provide an on-going income stream. Agents who work for only one insurance company (captive agents) sometimes are discouraged from selling term life because the commissions frequently stop being paid after a few years.

There is nothing inherently wrong with universal life and whole life. It is simply a matter of selecting the best policy that you can afford at that point in your life. Since money is frequently tight for many younger couples with minor children, term insurance is usually the preferred life insurance policy for them.

Fortunately, more insurance companies are making their policies available on-line. Since insurance agents are discouraged from selling term insurance due to the lower commissions, having the on-line option is frequently an excellent way to purchase term insurance.

EXAMPLE 4: According to one of the on-line companies mentioned later in this chapter, a person in good health can purchase a 30-year term life insurance policy with a $100,000 death benefit from a company rated A+ by A.M. Best for only $200 per year. Thirty-year term means that your annual premium will stay $200 for the entire 30-year period unless you stop paying the premium. Two hundred dollars per year is $16.57 per month or $3.85 per week (less than the cost of a Starbucks coffee).

Try to buy term life insurance when you are young and healthy since the premiums on new policies will increase as you get older. Plus, your health might worsen and coverage might be denied.

Universal life insurance

Universal life is a type of permanent life insurance which remains in place as long as premiums are paid either by the insured party or from the surplus (if any) in the cash value account. Universal life policies frequently have provisions in their contracts which enable the policyholder to modify the death benefit amount. This can enable the policy holder to adjust the existing contract without having to purchase a new policy.

EXAMPLE 5: Heather and Elizabeth are equal owners of a successful business. If one of them were to die, the remaining owner would quickly need funds to buy the deceased person's share from her heirs and to hire people to replace the owner who died. Heather and Elizabeth each take out a universal life policy that will fund a buy/sell agreement when one of the owners dies. They prefer using permanent insurance as opposed to term insurance since they do not anticipate selling the business. The universal life policies also have the ability to accept funds over and above the required premiums when business is good so that the cash value account can grow to cover the policy premiums if and when there is an economic slowdown, and it might be difficult to pay the premiums.

If you are considering buying universal life, look carefully at the projections. Several years ago, universal life policies assumed that higher interest rates would continue indefinitely. With rates for ten-year U.S. Treasury obligations now pay less than two percent, those overly optimistic projections are requiring that owners pay much higher premiums to keep the policy from collapsing (imploding).

Whole life insurance

Whole life insurance is similar to UL because it too is considered permanent as long as there are premiums being paid. There is no term. Unlike UL which offers flexible premiums, whole life has a set premium. Whole life is also commonly used to fund buy/sell agreements.

3. HOW TO BUY LIFE INSURANCE

Many people have life insurance coverage through their employer. As an employee benefit, it is group coverage which means that employees receive the benefit regardless of their health. People with serious health issues who might otherwise not qualify for life insurance or not be able to afford coverage, are able to be covered through the group policy of the employer.

At large companies, employees can frequently purchase additional insurance coverage. Insurance companies will compete for the business of the employer in order to get access to the employees who will hopefully buy additional coverage for themselves and their families.

We have prepared numerous estate plans for individuals who work for large companies and have taken advantage of opportunities to purchase supplement insurance. It has not been unusual for a couple with young children to have one million dollars of life insurance through the life insurance provider where one of the parents works.

If you do not have life insurance coverage through an employer, then you need to decide if you want individual coverage.

Relatively simple life insurance policies like term life can easily be purchased through on-line providers. Business insurance such as policies used to fund buy/sell agreements are far more complicated and should be purchased through experienced agents. Again, independent agents can offer policies from several companies whereas captive agents are usually required to sell only those policies of their employer.

Now there are several sources to purchase life insurance on-line. Some offer quotes from several different insurance companies while others only sell insurance from one company (AIG, Globe Life and Protective Life).

The following sources are provided in alphabetical order as examples and are not being endorsed by the authors:

Lifeplans.com	(844) 551-7586
Policygenius.com	(855) 695-2255
Selectquote.com	(800) 320-2956

In an effort to reduce their costs, companies are bypassing insurance agents by setting up websites where they offer their policies directly to potential buyers. Companies with direct sell websites include:

Aigdirect.com	(800) 294-4544
Globelifeinsurance.com	(800) 742-6787
Protective.com	(800) 866-9933

If you are comfortable working with sales representatives on-line, then consider using a company which provides quotes and processes applications via the internet. If you prefer more personal attention, then contact a local independent insurance agent. An independent agent represents multiple companies and should shop for the best policy for you. A captive insurance agent works for one company and is obligated (contractually or if the person wants to keep their job) to recommend the policies of their employer.

CHAPTER SUMMARY

Life insurance can be a cost-effective way of making sure that your wealth is not destroyed by your premature death. If you purchase life insurance, make sure the insurance company is financially stable by checking how they are rated on one of the major rating services.

Types of life insurance include term insurance, universal life insurance and whole life insurance. Term insurance is usually the best option for younger individuals with limited funds who want to cover obligations like mortgages and college education. Universal life and whole life are more suited for situations like business related transactions where there is likely to be a permanent need for life insurance which justifies the higher premium cost.

TAKE ACTION

- Add up the amount of debt you currently have and add future expenses you intend to cover like the projected cost of college education for your children. This number is the amount of life insurance you should consider buying if you can afford it.
- Decide what type of life insurance best fills your needs. Three common types of life insurance are term life insurance, universal life and whole life.
- Term life insurance is best for younger families seeking to cover debts and anticipated family expenses.
  - Go on-line and obtain life insurance quotes from more than one company. Specify that you want quotes from companies rated at A or better by A.M. Best. Ratings also include A+ and A++. If you have a complicated business-related insurance need, seek out the services of an experienced independent insurance agent.

Chapter 8 – Property Insurance

"Insurance is the only product that both the seller
and the buyer hope is never actually used."
Unknown

CHAPTER PREVIEW

Property insurance is a second tool you need to use to safeguard your assets as they GROW.

As you gain assets and wealth, you need to take steps to safeguard those assets. Property casualty insurance pays when an insured vehicle, house or other asset is damaged in an accident, fire or natural disaster.

If you have a mortgage on your house, then you probably have homeowner's insurance to safeguard the company that loaned you the money to buy your house. Should you owe $100,000 on a mortgage and your house burns down, the homeowner's insurance provides the funds to pay off the balance of the mortgage.

Car owners are required by most states to have car insurance. States want drivers to be insured to cover property damage they might cause as a result of a car accident as well as the health care costs of those injured in accidents.

In this chapter, we discuss three types of property insurance:
- Car insurance
- Real estate insurance
- Umbrella policies

1. CAR INSURANCE

States require that drivers have car insurance for the simple reason that a lot of people are involved in car accidents every year. The Federal Highway Administration recently estimated that more than six million car accidents occur each year in the United States. The number is probably higher since many accidents are never reported.

Most states want insurance available to provide compensation for injuries and pay for property damage resulting from car accidents. It is obviously fair that the person who is involved in an accident pays for damages either directly or indirectly through an insurance company. Otherwise, an innocent driver, passenger or pedestrian not only suffers from injuries caused by accidents but also has to pay for damage to their car or property because someone had no or inadequate car insurance.

When you apply for license plates, most states require that they produce proof that a vehicle owner has car insurance in place. Unfortunately, some people feel compelled to try to scam the system by dropping the insurance coverage shortly after getting licensed. Given how expensive car repairs are you should at least have the minimum amount required. There is also that matter of it being against the law to drive a car without a license and without insurance.

EXAMPLE 1: John plans to lease a new car and has been told by his salesperson that he will need to have car insurance in place before he will be able to drive the car home. John contacts an insurance agency used by his parents and purchases the amount of coverage required to lease the car.

Fortunately, safety measures in newer cars have reduced the number of motor vehicle deaths in recent years. The National Safety Council estimated that in 2019, approximately 38,000 people died in car accidents in the United States.

If you cannot afford car insurance, then you have lost the privilege of being able to drive. Find some alternative mode of transportation until you can afford insurance. If you were hit by a drunk driver, you would expect compensation for your injuries and property damage. Why should it be any different for someone else hit by your uninsured car?

When signing up for car insurance, you have to make decisions on the type and amount of coverage you want. In some cases, there is a minimum amount of insurance coverage required by the state where you declare your residency. The following information concerning the types of coverage comes from the Nationwide Mutual Insurance Company:

Collision Insurance

Damage to your car is covered by collision insurance in the event of a covered accident involving running into another vehicle. This may include repairs or a full replacement of your covered vehicle.

Comprehensive Insurance

Damage to your vehicle caused by covered events such as theft, vandalism or hail, which are not collision-related are paid for by comprehensive insurance.

Liability Insurance

Auto liability insurance covers the damage to other vehicles and injuries to other people that result from an accident caused by the insured individual. Bodily injury coverage covers medical costs, funeral expenses, lost income and pain and suffering of people injured by you. Property damage coverage reimburses accident victims for the repair or replacement of belongings damaged by you. This covers both someone else's car or property, for instances, if you hit a sign or house.

2. REAL ESTATE INSURANCE

Two types of real estate insurance are homeowner's insurance and renter's insurance. When you purchase a house using a mortgage, homeowners' insurance is required by the lender to protect their interest. If you have put 20% down on your house and a mortgage company lent you the remaining 80%, how will the mortgage company get their 80% back if fire destroys your house? Homeowners' insurance protects both you and the lender from economic loss as long as you have adequately insured the property.

EXAMPLE 2: Mary has agreed to purchase a house and plans to have a mortgage. At the real estate closing, Mary is required to produce proof that she has obtained homeowners insurance for the value of the house she is buying. The bank providing the mortgage wants to preserve their investment by making sure their collateral (Mary's house) is worth the amount she still owes them. If Mary neglects to keep the homeowner insurance in force, then the bank will take out their own insurance policy and charge Mary for the premium.

EXAMPLE 3. John is currently renting an apartment. A confirmed bachelor, his furniture is not expensive, but his computers, telephone, TV and other electronic equipment is state of the art and would make the National Security Agency jealous. John purchases renter insurance to cover the cost of replacing his computers and other equipment. As a renter, he is responsible for damage to his apartment that he causes so he purchases insurance to cover those costs.

3. UMBRELLA POLICIES

Sometimes the amount of damage from a car accident or house fire exceeds the coverage of your insurance policy. An umbrella policy provides additional coverage beyond the maximum coverage you carry with your car and homeowners' insurance.

You could increase the amount of both your car and home insurance but why do both? An umbrella policy can cover multiple types of personal property insurance and be more cost-effective.

EXAMPLE 4: Anne has both car and homeowner's insurance. But Anne is worried that if her car was in an accident where someone was severely injured or if a guest at her house was hurt, her liability coverage would not be adequate. Rather than increase liability coverage in both her car and homeowners' insurance, she instead purchases an umbrella policy which provides up to one million dollars ($1,000,000) of additional insurance after her other policies have paid out their maximum benefit.

CHAPTER SUMMARY

Property and casualty insurance could recover the cost of repairing your property that is damaged and also provide liability coverage for you if you injure someone accidentally. An umbrella insurance policy provides additional coverage beyond what you have for your car and real estate you own or rent. It is frequently more cost effective than increasing your car and home insurance for the same amount.

TAKE ACTION

- Once a year, ask the insurance agent or company representative handling your car and homeowner's insurance to review your coverage. Ask if changes should be made to offset rate increases or to fill gaps in your coverage.
- Review what homes have sold for in your neighborhood. Compare the amount of replacement coverage you have to the price of home. Adjust as needed.
- Purchase an umbrella liability policy if you want additional coverage but prefer not to pay for additional coverage for both your car and home. It is extremely unlikely you will exceed the coverage limits for both your car and home insurance.

Chapter 9 – Investment Insurance

"People should be more concerned with the return of
their principal than the return on their principal."
Will Rogers

CHAPTER PREVIEW

Investment insurance is a third way to safeguard your assets so they
will continue to GROW. Despite what some investors believe, not all
investments are safe. That would seem like an obvious statement, but
millions of people are scammed every year by crooks and unethical
salespeople who promise sky-high returns with little or no risk.

You may have heard the Better Business Bureau saying: "If it
sounds too good to be true, it usually is." When presented with an
exceptional investment opportunity always ask yourself: "Why is this
particular financial product paying so much more than supposedly
similar investments?" Equally important, ask yourself: "How did I get
to be so lucky to be able to invest in this fantastic opportunity that
nobody else knows about?"

Would you buy a new Corvette for $10,000 (cash only in small
bills) from a private party when the same new Corvette is selling for
over $70,000 by established car dealers with showrooms and
employees? Why are you so fortunate to be picked to take advantage
of this $10,000 deal of a lifetime?

Hopefully, you would turn down obvious scams. But convicted
con man Bernie Madoff was able to get thousands of intelligent
people to invest in his multi-billion-dollar fraudulent operations
because he offered returns that were superior to other investment
advisors. Greed is an extremely powerful force.

At the Wall Street Zoo, bulls are positive that markets will go up
and bears are negative and are expecting the markets to drop. But
when it comes to being greedy, a favorite saying on Wall Street is:
"Bulls and bears make money, but pigs get slaughtered."

Once you have begun to accumulate assets like bank accounts and mutual funds, then logically you should want to make sure that you do not lose it all.

For those assets that you want more secure from loss, you should check out investments that offer some type of insurance. But understand how the insurance works, what is covered and how solid is the insurance.

In this chapter, three types of insurance which cover investments will be discussed:
- Deposit insurance
- State insurance guaranty funds
- Securities company insurance

1. DEPOSIT INSURANCE

In Chapter 1 (Emergency Savings Accounts), we recommended setting up a simple savings account funded with automatic deposits. Most people will find credit unions and banks to be easier to work with to start those savings accounts than with an alternative like a money market mutual fund.

In addition to being easy to set up and frequently (but not always) are free of fees, savings accounts at banks and credit unions are usually insured by agencies created by the federal government. Bank deposits are insured through the FDIC (Federal Deposit Insurance Corporation). Credit union accounts are backed by the NCUA (National Credit Union Association). Details about what deposits are covered by these agencies is explained below.

FDIC – Federal Deposit Insurance Corporation

Many people are familiar with FDIC bank insurance. But not all banks are FDIC insured. Same with credit unions. Not all participate in the NCUA. If you are investing in order to take advantage of insurance, make sure the institution is participating and the investments are properly set up to be fully insured.

CDs (Certificates of Deposit) are not all insured by either the FDIC or NCUA. Shortly before they declared bankruptcy, Lehman Brothers issued CDs backed by their company. You have many secure financial institutions to work with so stick with CDs and accounts that are FDIC or NCUA insured.

FDIC (Federal Deposit Insurance Corporation) backs deposits at U.S. banks. Bankers will frequently mention that deposits are insured up to $250,000 per account. The FDIC charges banks a fee which is used to fund the pool that pays out money when banks collapse, as many did in 2008 and 2009. As long as your funds (accounts and CDs) at a bank are equal to or less than $250,000, then the FDIC safeguards your deposits.

You can increase your insurance protection to over $250,000 through the use of joint names and by depositing funds in accounts like IRAs and trust accounts. If you are fortunate enough to have over $250,000, then make sure you use accounts that are insured or move the funds over $250,000 to another insured institution where those accounts will also be covered up to $250,000.

EXAMPLE 1: Debbie is the acting successor trustee of her deceased mother's trust. Debbie recently received a $300,000 check from a company where her mother had a life insurance policy. Debbie deposits the check into an account in the trust's name but as soon as the check clears, moves $75,000 to another bank (separate institution) since the trust account held over $250,000. Since the accounts (checking, savings and CDs) together are now less than $250,000 at each bank, the trust is taking full advantage of the FDIC insurance coverage.

But what happens if the FDIC pool runs out of money? Fortunately, the FDIC has the legal authority to borrow funds from the United States Treasury. Some people might argue that with the national debt at 10 trillion dollars and growing after the most recent tax cut, the backing by the U.S. Treasury is hardly comforting. But the United States of America is still the world's largest and probably strongest economy, so the guarantee is solid. Do not be deceived into thinking that all investment products sold by bankers are FDIC insured. Frequently, higher yielding products offered at banks are annuities that are issued by insurance companies. Banks like them because the insurance companies pay the bank a fat commission to sell these products to their clients who are seeking alternatives to low-rate CDs.

There are FDIC-backed hybrid CDs which are issued by larger banks. FDIC coverage extends to $250,000 like other bank deposits. However, unlike traditional CDs which have a fixed rate of interest for the term of the CD, hybrid CDs pay based on the performance of some index or basket of stocks.

EXAMPLE 2: Fred is retired and wants to keep a substantial portion of his funds in FDIC backed investments. He is unhappy with the low rate of interest currently being offered at banks, but he is concerned about investing more money in the stock markets. Fred's investment advisor recommends a hybrid CD whose rate of return is linked to five well-known stocks. Every year, on the date the CD was issued, if the closing share price of all five stocks are equal to or even slightly higher than their share price on the issue date, then Fred will receive a cash payment of 6%. If the share price of any of the five stocks is less than their share price on the issue date, then Fred will receive a much lower money market rate. The attraction of hybrid CDs is that, unlike a direct investment in the five stocks, the FDIC backing will preserve the principal if the share price of any of the five stocks drop.

While hybrid CDs have the potential of providing a higher return than traditional fixed rate CDs, hybrid CDs are more complicated and require additional disclosure about the return being calculated. Make sure that the hybrid CD is FDIC backed and that the formula used to calculate the return is easy to understand and confirm to know that you received what you are entitled to.

NCUA – National Credit Union Administration

Just as the Federal Deposit Insurance Corporation covers insured bank accounts up to $250,000 from bank failure, the National Credit

Union Administration (NCUA) covers insured credit union accounts also up to $250,000 from credit union failure.

FDIC and NCUA Limits

Should you be fortunate enough to have over $250,000 in combined checking and savings (including CD's) at any one bank or credit union, you can increase your deposit insurance coverage by having different names on your accounts or by moving funds to a different financial institution. As we will be discussing in Chapter 20 (Avoiding Probate) joint deposit accounts can have unexpected problems related to ownership and who inherits the funds. With so many financial institutions with local branches and online access, moving funds to a different bank or credit union frequently is the best option, regardless of what the friendly customer service people tell you at the institution about to lose the funds.

If you want your deposits to be fully insured by the FDIC or NCUA but you dislike keeping track of multiple accounts, consider investing in CDs through an investment account. Many banks will offer their CDs through a brokerage account. Why not? It enables an institution to reach potential depositors where they have no branches and provides depositors with the opportunity to secure CDs rates in other parts of the U.S. which might be higher than what is offered by their local banks. Make sure if you go this route that the CDs are backed by the FDIC or NCUA and that you never exceed the $250,000 limit at any one financial institution, regardless of the interest rate and how clever the bank's commercials are.

2. STATE INSURANCE GUARANTY FUNDS

All states have some type of pool or association which provides a limited amount of coverage in event an insurance company has financial difficulties and declares bankruptcy.

Unlike the FDIC for banks and NCUA for credit unions, the state insurance guaranty funds are not backed by the federal government. In the event of a liquidity crisis, the FDIC and NCUA are able to apply for loans from the U.S. Treasury. Instead of being backed by an agency of the Federal Government, state guaranty funds are supported by the insurance companies that are doing business in a particular state.

Even without federal backing, state guaranty associations have provided substantial payouts. According to NOLHGA, since 1983, state guaranty associations have contributed "approximately $8.97 billion towards the fulfillment of insurer promises."

EXAMPLE 3: Fred is a conservative investor who traditionally has kept most of his money in CDs at banks to take advantage of the FDIC insurance. Fred is contacted by an insurance agent seeking to sell Fred an annuity. When Fred indicates his preference for FDIC insured deposits, Fred's insurance agent says that annuities are backed by funds provided by the insurance companies doing business in that state. Fred buys a $50,000 annuity based on that information.

Ask yourself if you feel more comfortable with your assets being backed by the full faith and credit of the United States or by the assets of insurance companies that have chosen to conduct business in your state. Even with trillion-dollar deficits, most people would agree that the insurance provided by the FDIC and NCUA with the backing of the U.S. Treasury is far stronger than the state guaranty agencies which have no government backing.

Hopefully investment insurance is never needed. But credit unions and banks have failed due to bad loans and mismanagement. Make sure your assets are safeguarded.

3. SECURITIES COMPANY INSURANCE

What happens to investors when the securities company holding their investments goes bankrupt? Whether due to mismanagement or fraud, the Securities Investor Protection Corporation (SIPC) provides insurance coverage for investments held at securities companies. It is important to note that the SPIC does not insure against market loss. If you invest in DogFood.com which goes bankrupt, you eat the loss.

But if the company holding your investments goes bankrupt, you could be covered.

SIPC – Securities Investor Protection Corporation

The FDIC and NCUA covers deposits at insured bank and credit union accounts. The Securities Investor Protection Corporation (SIPC) backs securities (stocks, bonds, mutual funds, etc.) held at insured brokerage firms that have financial difficulties have closed or are in danger of closing.

According to the SIPC website (sipc.com): "SIPC protects against the loss of cash and securities – such as stocks and bonds – held by a customer at a financially-troubled SIPC-member brokerage firm. The limit of SIPC coverage is $500,000, which includes a $250,000 limit for cash. Most customers of failed brokerage firms have insurance coverage through SIPC when assets are missing from customer accounts."

What SIPC does NOT cover is a loss of market value. Again, from the SIPC website (sipc.com): "SIPC does not protect against the decline in value of your investments. SIPC does not protect individuals who were sold worthless stocks and other securities. SIPC does not protect claims against a broker for bad advice, or for recommending inappropriate investments."

EXAMPLE 4:   Fred utilizes the services of Paul, an investment advisor whose broker-dealer is Matrix Investment, Inc. Paul moved to Matrix because they claimed to have technology that Paul felt would greatly help him serve his clients. Fred moved his investments to Matrix when his advisor became affiliated with Matrix. When the economy goes into a recession, Matrix Investments, Inc. has financial difficulties and declares bankruptcy. SPIC covers Fred's investments to the maximum allowed.

CHAPTER SUMMARY

Deposit insurance covers your checking and savings accounts as well as CDs you have at banks or credit unions that are insured by either the FDIC (banks) or the NCUA (credit unions). State insurance guarantee funds provide an additional potential source of repayment if an insurance company you are dealing with goes bankrupt. State guaranty funds are not backed by any federal agency and are instead supported by insurance companies doing business in a particular state. Securities company insurance safeguards the assets you have with a particular broker dealer. SPIC does not prevent you from incurring market losses.

TAKE ACTION

- Keep the majority of your transaction accounts (checking and savings) with institutions which are backed either by the FDIC (banks) or the NCA (credit unions). If you prefer to write checks from a brokerage account, make sure the institution holding your funds is financially secure.
- If state insurance covering your annuities is important to you, check with the appropriate state agency as to how much coverage the state agency provides. Only invest in annuities from financially secure companies so that you do not have to rely on the state insurance.
- Whenever you are investing through a financial advisor, inquire as to if the company they work for is backed by the SIPC. When at their office, see if a SIPC sign is displayed. Also ask which firm the advisor uses as the custodian for your investments.

Part II: How to **Employ** Wealth

PREVIEW OF PART II - EMPLOY

Money needs to work for you so treat your assets like a valued employee. Employ is defined by the Cambridge Dictionary as: "To use something for a particular purpose." Money has no real value unless it is spent (used) – hopefully wisely.

Part Two of this book discusses how to employ your money to work harder for you by spending less on taxes, controlling your debts and better managing the income you receive in retirement.

SECTION CHAPTERS

Financial Management

Financial management requires action. People who pay for an expensive financial plan that never gets implemented have wasted their valuable time and money. Become a better financial manager and you will employ your assets to move you ever closer to your goal and destination of financial independence.

Section One: Minimize Your Taxes

Chapter 10 – Income Taxes

*"Anyone may arrange his affairs so that his taxes shall be
as low as possible; he is not bound to choose the pattern
which will best pay the Treasury; there is not even a patriotic
duty to increase one's taxes."*
Judge Learned Hand

MINIMIZE YOUR TAXES

Section One on how to EMPLOY your wealth covers legal ways
to MINIMIZE YOUR TAXES to have more money working for you.
The taxes we will focus on are: 1) Income taxes; 2) Property taxes;
and 3) Death taxes.

CHAPTER PREVIEW

*Income taxes are the first category of taxes you should seek to
minimize.*

In the United States, we have a progressive tax system at the
federal level. As your income goes up, you "progress" (the verb) into
the next higher tax bracket and are given the opportunity to send more
to the IRS. Some people do not view that as "progress" (the noun).

The current Federal income tax rates for individuals (see below)
are 10%, 12%, 22%, 24%, 32%, 35% and 37%. If you are in the 22%
tax bracket, you send the IRS 22% of your income that is subject to
taxation at that rate. Add your state income tax rate (if any) to the
federal rate and you have your effective tax rate.

Some politicians and economists have proposed that the U.S. adopt
a flat income tax instead of the current progressive tax system.
Everyone would pay say 25 % on all their income whether they made
$50,000 a year or $800,000 yearly.

The problem with a flat tax would be that politicians would never let it remain simple and flat. Washington lobbyists (who are frequently retired or defeated politicians) are paid huge sums to get tax breaks for clients. Given how much politicians are willing to spend on getting elected, tax simplicity would quickly be abandoned in exchange for campaign contributions.

Since it is highly likely our progressive Federal tax system is here to stay, to GET Wealth, you need to learn how to legally minimize your income tax burden. Pay the IRS what you should, not what you could.

In this chapter, the following three aspects of income taxes will be discussed:
- Tax brackets
- Tax deductions
- Tax deferral

1. TAX BRACKETS

You can draw a lot of blank expressions from people by asking "What is your current tax bracket?" This should not be a minefield question like: "How much money do you make?" or "Is that your real hair and color?" or "Before you eat those three corn dogs, how much do you weigh"?

As we explained above, your tax bracket is the percentage of your income you pay in taxes. Therefore, if you are in the 22% tax bracket, you pay 22% of your ordinary income to the IRS.

As a general rule, if you make less money, your tax bracket is low (10% or 12%). Middle income earners are usually in the 22% or 24% tax bracket. Congratulations if you are in the 32%, 35% or 37% tax brackets which entitles you to a mumbled thank you every time Congress passes a new spending bill.

Your friends are about to name you The Tax Guru. Here are the individual federal tax rates for 2021 which determine your tax bracket:

Table A: Single taxpayers

Taxable Income	Tax Rate
$0 to $9,950	10%
$9,951 to $40,525	12%
$40,526 to $86,375	22%
$86,376 to $164,925	24%
$164,926 to $209,425	32%
$209,426 to $523,600	35%
Over $523,600	37%

Table B: Married filing jointly

Taxable Income	Tax Rate
$0 to $19,900	10%
$19,901 to $81,050	12%
$81,051 to $172,750	22%
$172,751 to $329,850	24%
$329,851 to $418,850	32%
$418,851 to $628,350	35%
Over $628,350	37%

Table C: Heads of Households

Taxable Income	Tax Rate
$0 to $14,200	10%
$14,201 to $54,200	12%
$54,201 to $86,350	22%
$86,351 to $164,900	24%
$164,901 to $209,400	32%
$209,401 to $523,600	35%
Over $523,600	37%

EXAMPLE 1: Judy is single and earns $60,000 of taxable income per year. According to TABLE A above, a single taxpayer with taxable income between $40,526 and $86,375 would be in the 22% tax bracket. As your taxable income increases, you potentially move

into the next highest tax bracket. If Judy earns taxable income of $90,000, her income between $40,526 and $86,375 would be taxed at 22% while her taxable income over $86,375 would be taxed at 24%.

EXAMPLE 2: Lucy and Ricky are married and together earn $75,000 of taxable income. TABLE B above indicates that a married couple earning taxable income between $19,901 and $81,050 are in the 12% bracket. If Lucy and Ricky were to earn $85,000, their taxable income between $19,901 and $81,050 would be taxed at 12% while their taxable income over $81,051 will be taxed at 22%.

As we discussed in Chapter 2 (Tax-Favored Assets), taxpayers in the two lowest tax brackets (10% and 12%) pay zero federal taxes on qualified dividends and long-term capital gains. Where possible, managing the amount of taxable income you receive from sources like investments and discretionary IRA distributions can have a substantial impact on how much you send the IRS.

At the annual half-way mark (July 4th – Independence Day), review your income projections for the rest of the year. Your financial independence depends on taking steps to legally minimize your income taxes.

2. TAX DEDUCTIONS

Once you know your tax bracket and unofficially designate yourself as a CFG (Certified Financial Guru), how can you legally minimize your income taxes to pay only your fair share? One word: deductions. Another word that would also minimize your income taxes would be to take up "slacking" but that would not be in keeping with the intent of this book to GET Wealth.

Tax deductions reduce the amount of money that is subject to tax. You can either take a standard deduction or itemize your deductions. In 2019, the standard deduction was doubled so fewer taxpayers are taking the time to itemize their deductions. For 2021, the standard deduction is $12,550 for single taxpayers, $25,100 for joint filers and $18,800 for heads of households.

EXAMPLE 3: Fred used to itemize his income tax deductions. For 12 months he would meticulously keep every paid bill that he thought he might be able to deduct as a business expense. When preparing his taxes, Fred would dump the box containing all these bills, slips of paper, napkins with notes on them, etc. on a table and proceed to total up his "business deductions." After spending countless hours recording potential expenses, Fred figured he could deduct about 20% of the bills he had saved. Not the best use of his time (as mentioned by his spouse every year). The higher standard deduction (fortunately) eliminated the annual "dumping of the tax receipt box" for many taxpayers.

Itemizing deductions sometimes has the effect of encouraging "creative accounting" when deciding what could be a deduction. One person claimed a property loss deduction for storm damage to a tree in his backyard every year on several tax returns, even after the tree was cut down. Please do not underestimate the sophistication of the taxpayer-financed IRS computers which monitor tax returns.

3. TAX DEFERRAL

If you cannot eliminate a tax, the next best option is to delay paying it until a more favorable time.

For example, suppose you are a single taxpayer earning taxable income of $90,000. According to the previous tax tables, you are in the 24% tax bracket. An additional $100 of taxable income would be reduced by 24% or $24. Instead of taking the additional $100 as income and giving up $24 for taxes, you have the $100 put into your 401(k) plan. Since deposits into a 401(k) are "pre-tax" the entire $100 is invested, without the $24 (24%) tax haircut.

Where does tax deferral come to the rescue? Funds invested in a 401(k) plan are not taxed until they come out of the 401(k) plan. The income taxes are not eliminated. The taxes are deferred.

Again, in the above example, assume you retire when you are 67 years old. As a retiree, you no longer earn taxable income of $90,000. Instead with Social Security and investment income, your taxable income is now $40,000 per year. Again, according to the above tax table, at $40,000, you are now in the 12% tax bracket.

CHAPTER SUMMARY

Tax brackets indicate the percentage of your taxable income that you owe the IRS. As your income goes up, so does the amount you pay in federal taxes. Tax deductions reduce your taxable income. When you lower your taxable income, you might also lower your tax bracket. Tax deferral postpones the year that you will owe income taxes on an investment. Defer until you are in a lower tax bracket (like retirement) so that you pay less in income taxes.

TAKE ACTION

- Determine your current tax bracket by comparing your taxable income reported on your last federal tax return with the appropriate Table A, B or C above.
- Compare the standard deduction you receive automatically with a list of large, itemized deductions. If you do not have substantial deductions, do not waste the time and effort to itemize.
- If it is likely that you will be in a lower tax bracket in the future, most likely after you retire, try to defer as much income as you can until your tax bracket drops. Investing pre-tax funds in retirement accounts or after-tax funds in tax-deferred annuities are some of the most common ways to accomplish this goal.

Chapter 11 – Property Taxes

"I hate paying taxes. But I love the civilization they gave me."
Oliver Wendell Holmes

CHAPTER PREVIEW

Property taxes are a second group of taxes you should work to minimize to increase the funds you have available to EMPLOY.

No homeowner looks forward to paying property taxes. But assuming they are spent wisely, property taxes can have a great impact on the value of your home.

Property taxes support critical local services like public schools along with police and fire protection. How likely will it be for someone to buy your house if the local schools are considered way below average and your neighborhood is experiencing high crime levels due to poor police protection?

Since property taxes are based on the perceived value of your home, vacation house and/or commercial buildings, you need to make sure you are paying your fair share of property taxes, no more, no less. To GET (Grow, Employ and Transfer) Wealth, you need to spend your money wisely, including what you pay for property taxes.

In this chapter, the following aspects of property taxes will be discussed:
- Property tax uses
- Property tax assessments
- Appealing property tax assessments

1. PROPERTY TAX USES

In addition to funding schools and paying for essential services like police and fire protection, property taxes help provide for local parks, water and sewer services, community colleges and a wide variety of local government services. Property taxes not only pay for services directly, but they also are used to pay interest on and redeem municipal bonds that are issued to construct buildings and make improvements to roads and water systems.

EXAMPLE 1: The Lakeshore School District wanted to construct a new high school since the community had grown substantially and the current building was overcrowded. The school board asked voters in the school district to authorize a $30 million bond issue to raise funds to construct and furnish a new building. The voters approved the bond issue, and the municipal bonds were purchased by investors who will be paid back interest and their principal over 25 years with higher property taxes imposed on property owners in the school district. The new building was constructed with the bond proceeds and has been viewed as a very positive addition to the community.

While funding schools and other local services is critically important, homeowners should take the time to learn what portion of their property tax bills are going for each project and service.

Government entities (school districts, counties, cities, townships, etc.) will frequently ask voters to approve "mileages" to maintain or expand schools, roads or continue services. If you own property, do you fully understand the cumulative effect of these taxes?

When you are buying an expensive new car, salespeople have been trained to tell you the monthly payment for a lease or loan rather than the total cost per year. The idea is to close the sale by making the cost appear smaller by focusing on the monthly payment.

The same approach is sometimes taken when "selling" a millage to property owners. A new proposed tax is presented as being "only" an additional two mills or $2 for every $1,000 of taxable value. Cheap except that the proposed millage will increase taxes by $200 for a house valued at $100,000.

According to Zillow, in May 2021, the average price of a home in the United States was $287,148, up 13.2% in one year. Two mills does not sound like a lot but as the value of the property increases, so does your tax bill.

Years ago, Illinois Senator Everett Dirksen responded to someone trying to minimize the cost of a new government project by saying: "A billion here and a billion there and pretty soon you are talking about big money." A mill here and a mill there and soon you have a large property tax bill.

Now the Federal government passes multi trillion-dollar programs and the only complaints from taxpayers are that the approved programs did not adequately fund things they felt were important. We need to make sure our (property) taxes are going for services and projects that will increase the value of our property and provide the environment you want and are able to afford.

2. PROPERTY TAX ASSESSMENTS

Property taxes start with a property tax assessment. What do the local tax assessors feel your property is worth? The higher the value, the more tax you pay. A one mill (one percent) tax on a home with a taxable value of $100,000 is obviously less than the same one mil (one percent) tax on a house with a taxable value of $300,000.

This is not a problem unless the house with a taxable value of $100,000 really should have an assessed taxable value of $150,000 and the house with the $300,000 taxable value instead should be assessed at $250,000. Taxes need to be fair to all, not just those who pay the least.

Once a year, homeowners receive a document indicating what the assessors feel the taxable value of your house should be for the coming tax year. When you receive it, do you review it or just stick it in the drawer with other important papers like pizza coupons?

Make sure your property is being correctly assessed. Compare what the local tax assessors are claiming your house is worth vs what your neighbors are listing and selling their homes for. If similar houses in your area are selling for substantially more than what your property is being assessed, then this would be a good time to demonstrate just how silent you can be around your local assessors. If the presumed value of your three bedroom, two bath house is being assessed like an ocean-front mansion in Miami, Florida, then you need to consider challenging the valuation.

EXAMPLE 2: Mary and Sam own a three-bedroom colonial in a nice neighborhood. After checking the records at their local assessor, they learn that three similar sized houses on their street have taxable values more than $20,000 less than their home. After presenting documents to the local assessor, they try proving that the square footage of their house was incorrect. The taxable value was reduced to correspond to other comparable homes and their property tax bill was adjusted downward.

Have you ever challenged your property tax assessment? It is non undignified to question your local property tax assessor if you truly believe they have assessed your house as being worth far more than you could possibly sell it for. Unless you are that rare individual who takes great pride in paying the most property taxes of anyone on your street on the premise that means you have the nicest home, pay your fair share of taxes, no more and no less.

Most states are broken down into counties. In Michigan, for example, there are 83 counties. Each State determines the value of the property in a particular country. Then the county breaks down the value of the property in each city, village, township, etc. in that county. A fine example of the trickle- down effect only this time to calculate your property taxes.

Now suppose the local assessor is aware that you just put in a new kitchen in your house. Forget that your previous kitchen had cabinets that looked like they came from a garage sale. Forget that your kitchen is 12 X 12, and your neighbor has a panty that large in a kitchen they updated five years ago but the owners' friend of a friend/carpenter "forgot" to pull any building permits.

Your friendly assessor now determines that your house is worth more due to the extensive renovations that you did.

Whether you own a house or rent an apartment, you are paying property taxes. If you are a homeowner, you get to pay property either directly to the local tax authorities or the company which handles your mortgage which will include approximately one-twelfth $(1/12^{th})$ of the required annual taxes in your tax bill.

Pay your own property taxes and get a receipt confirming they were paid. Given concerns about mail delivery, it might be advisable to pay your property taxes in person where you can request a date-stamped receipt showing when they processed the payments. If you mail in your payment, you run the risk that the check gets lost and you will incur penalties for late payment. When filing your income taxes, you should have proof not only that your property taxes were paid but that they were paid on a particular date.

Dates are important. For example, your winter tax bill might say that the taxes are not "due" until February 15 of the following year. But if you wait an extra six weeks to collect all that income you made at the current .0001 percent interest rate being paid by The Biggie Banks, you cannot take the tax deduction in the prior year. You now have to wait until the following year to get a potential refund based on the property taxes you paid.

Free Advice: Do not pay property taxes with a credit card where transaction fees are charged.

Some communities will impose a five percent fee for you to charge your property taxes. Rarely is a credit card company going to pay you anywhere near five percent in cash rebates or airline miles.

3. APPEALING PROPERTY ASSESSMENTS

If you feel your property has been valued too high for tax purposes, you have the right to appeal. Property that has been assessed too high will result in a property tax bill that is also too high.

Since property taxes are imposed based on the value of your home, the most common reason for an appeal is that the current value of your house is much lower than what the local property accessor claims.

EXAMPLE 3: John and Mary purchased a three-bedroom house five years ago when the housing market was extremely strong. Due to a major slowdown in the economy, several local employers have laid off workers and housing prices have dropped significantly. John does not feel his house is worth what the tax assessors claim based on the prices people are asking for several unsold houses in his neighborhood. He challenges the assessment and armed with data about the lower prices that have been accepted for houses similar to his, he receives a slight reduction in the assessment of his home.

If you are going to claim you are being overcharged for property taxes, you first have to know what other comparable homes in your community are being assessed. The closer a comparable house is to your house the better. Do not try to compare your 3,000 square foot, four-bedroom, twelve-bathroom house built ten years ago with a 900 square foot, two-bedroom, shotgun house three miles away that borders on railroad tracks and was built by homesteaders before statehood.

Be realistic. Despite what your sixth-grade teacher said about you in speech class, your powers of persuasion are not that good to get assessors to agree that totally different houses are comparable. If your appeal is rejected by the local assessing board, do not give up unless your claim was so bogus that even you could get through your presentation without laughing.

It will get more expensive as you move up the chain of appeals. If you feel the stakes are high enough, you could hire an attorney. Make sure you hire a real estate attorney who is familiar with property tax appeals. Just because a lawyer advertises on cable TV at 3:00 a.m., does not mean they are a good fit to handle a property tax appeal. If possible, ask people who own multiple properties who they use for their real estate assessment issues.

CHAPTER SUMMARY

Property taxes are used to pay for local schools, police and fire protection, water and sewer maintenance and local government services. Property tax assessments determine the taxable value of dwellings, buildings and vacant property. Appealing property assessments is the process of seeking a reduction in the taxable value that has been assigned to your real property.

TAKE ACTION

- Determine from your most recent property tax bills what millage rate you are paying for each of the services being funded.
- Visit your local assessing department to ask to see how other homes similar to yours in your neighborhood are assessed.
- If you feel that your property is being assessed for substantially more than it is worth compared to other similar properties, then pursue an appeal first with your local authorities and then your state tax authority if you believe the amounts at stake are substantial.

Chapter 12 – Death Taxes

"In this world nothing can be said to be certain,
except death and taxes."
Ben Franklin

CHAPTER PREVIEW

Death taxes are a third group of taxes you should work to minimize as you EMPLOY your wealth.

Estate taxes are frequently referred to as death taxes because, when owed, they are imposed when someone dies, and assets are transferred to someone else.

"Death Taxes" sound more negative than "estate taxes" which helps the marketing efforts by those people who want to abolish all taxes triggered when someone dies. One reason for ending estate taxes is that they do not generate a great deal of revenue, given that very few people actually pay death taxes. The opponents of death taxes also point out that people usually paid income taxes as their wealth grew so why should they have to pay again to transfer their assets to whoever they want?

In this chapter, the following concepts involving estate taxes will be discussed:
- Estate tax rates
- Stepped up cost basis
- State inheritance taxes

1. ESTATE TAX RATES

For a change, how about some good news regarding taxes? Since 1982 there has been an unlimited marital deduction so there is no cap on the amount you can give your spouse without incurring Federal estate or gift taxes. You could be a multi-billionaire and if you leave all your assets to your spouse, no Federal estate or gift tax will be owed.

The amount you can transfer Federal tax-free to individuals other than your spouse has gone up substantially over the past 20 years. For 2021, the Unified Estate and Gift Tax Exclusion is $11,700,000. Translated to English, each person can give up to $11,700,000 to individuals other than their spouse without having to pay Federal estate or gift taxes. Congress has effectively eliminated Federal transfer taxes for an estimated 99.5% of American taxpayers.

But wait! Similar to some cable TV commercials airing at 3:00 a.m., for a limited time only, the deal gets better! Married couples are able to combine the $11.7 million Federal estate tax exemption given each spouse so that together they effectively pass double the amount, over $23 million (again indexed for inflation) to their children, grandchildren or other individuals without incurring Federal estate or gift taxes. This is called portability.

By exempting so many people from having to pay an estate tax, the tax planning aspect of estate planning has become much simpler and easier to understand. This has also reduced the complexity of preparing revocable trusts since estate taxes are rarely an issue. Because the estate taxes are no longer an issue for most Americans, the cost of preparing an estate plan has gone down. If you are considering hiring an attorney to prepare your estate planning documents, make sure you are not being charged as if estate tax computations are still required.

It is estimated that less than one-quarter of one percent (.25%) of Americans will now be subject to federal estate taxes. Even then, if someone has an estate worth over $11 million, they can afford to hire advisors who will structure their assets and prepare estate plans to enable them to pay little or no estate taxes.

Since most Americans will no longer owe federal estate taxes and/or state inheritance or estate taxes, your estate plan should be far less complex than estate plans your affluent grandparents or parents had before the estate tax exemption was raised so dramatically. To avoid federal estate taxes which once kicked in at $250,000 or less, estate planners used to prepare documents that included marital trusts, family trusts, generation-skipping trusts and a menu of trusts going by acronyms like: GRATs, SLATs, CRUTs, etc.

If you have estate planning documents that were done years ago when a much lower tax threshold was in place, dust off your documents and review them yourself or pay to have them reviewed by an estate planning attorney. The lawyer who arranges your bail bonds probably is not a good choice. You might be able to amend your documents to take advantage of the new tax laws and greatly simplify your estate plan.

EXAMPLE 1: Michelle and Jason are married and have three children and two grandchildren. Michelle and Jason had estate plans prepared 10 years ago which included both a marital trust and a family trust in order to avoid federal estate taxes. Since their combined net worth is under $5 million, they have signed new documents which leave all assets to the surviving spouse and then transfer the assets to their surviving children or grandchildren upon the death of the surviving spouse.

While the current federal estate tax exemption is $11,700,000, the 2017 law had a sunset provision which will scale back the estate tax exemption to approximately $5 million (adjusted for inflation) on January 1, 2026, unless Congress makes the higher level permanent before then. While this may look like an effort to keep estate planning attorneys employed to make changes, this is a federal budget matter. It also enables politicians to collect campaign contributions from lobbyists either advocating or opposing the higher federal estate tax exemption. The opera is not over.

The elimination of federal estate taxes for most American taxpayers has made estate planning less complicated for estates under $5,000,000 but has increased the need for income tax planning.

It is now relatively easy to avoid estate taxes. But the transfer of assets has become more complicated due to the increased use of IRAs and the increasing number of "blended" families which are the result of second and third marriages with children, grandchildren and a collection of heirs that make The Adams Family look normal.

2. STEPPED-UP COST BASIS

By eliminating federal estate taxes on $11,700,000 of assets for an individual, the ability to minimize death taxes has been greatly simplified. However, there are still income taxes that someone could incur when they inherit assets. Withdrawals from a traditional IRA are tax-deferred so beneficiaries of traditional IRA will owe income taxes on those assets.

Stepped-up cost basis provides an important way to avoid income taxes on inherited assets. At death, certain assets of the deceased adjust to the value of those assets on the date of death of the deceased. The gains on those assets which would have been taxed had they been sold during the lifetime of the owner, are now buried along with the deceased.

EXAMPLE 2: Sue is a single person who spent $5,000 to purchase 100 shares of ATX, Inc. several years ago at $50 per share (100 shares times $50 per share equals $5,000). The cost basis of the stock is set at $50 per share or $5,000 of value. Stock in ATX, Inc. has gone up substantially and is currently selling at $900 per share (100 shares times $900 per share equals $90,000). If Sue were to sell her 100 shares of ATX, Inc. at $900 per share, she would owe income tax on the gain of $85,000 ($90,000 proceeds from the sale at $900 per share minus the $5,000 purchase cost equals a gain of $85,000). Sue owns the stock at the time of her death. The IRS allows the new cost basis to "step up" from the original $50 per share to the current $900 per share. If the shares are sold for $900 per share, there is no gain and no income tax owed.

Stepped-up cost basis can provide very substantial income tax savings if done properly. Assets like stocks, mutual funds, real estate and ETFs qualify for stepped up basis treatment. IRAs, annuities and CDs do not. Taking more than the Required Minimum Distribution from your IRA and investing in assets which are eligible for the stepped-up cost basis could be an effective way to transfer more to your heirs with less income taxes imposed on the gains you may have otherwise realized.

3. STATE INHERITANCE TAXES

While federal estate taxes have been eliminated for over 99.5% of all Americans, certain states impose death taxes on their residents. Estate taxes are imposed on the giver (the estate of the deceased) while inheritance taxes are paid by the receiver (beneficiary).

The 12 states which tax estates are: Connecticut, Hawaii, Illinois, Maine, Maryland, Massachusetts, Minnesota, New York, Oregon, Rhode Island, Vermont and Washington. The six states which tax inheritances are: Iowa, Kentucky, Maryland, Nebraska, New Jersey and Pennsylvania. The tax rates vary as do the rules as to who is subject to taxation, so it is best to check with a local CPA who handles estate tax returns.

To avoid state estate and inheritance taxes, wealthy individuals frequently become residents of states without these taxes. But before you go through the time and expense to become a resident of another state, check to see if you are currently exempt from those taxes. Exemptions from state taxes vary greatly. New York exempts the first $5.74 million from their state estate tax while nearby Massachusetts only exempts $1 million from their state estate tax.

EXAMPLE 3: Sarah and Fred are a retired married couple who are residents of Massachusetts. Their combined assets are approximately $4 million so together, they would not be subject to a federal estate tax (each worth less than $11,700,000) but they are over the $1 million Massachusetts State estate tax exemption each of them is entitled to. Since they already own a condo in Tampa, Florida to escape snowy winter weather, they decide to become residents of Florida and thereby avoid the state estate tax imposed by Massachusetts.

Only changing your driver's license to show that you now reside in a lower tax state is probably not enough to prevent the state where you used to reside to give up trying to collect taxes from you. If you split your time between your new tax haven and your former principal residence in a high-tax state, be prepared to defend yourself from claims that you still owe estate taxes to your former state.

In states without an inheritance tax, it is common to have real estate agents, attorneys, CPA's, investment advisors, etc. host seminars touting the tax advantages to moving to their state. In Florida, local newspapers frequently have ads promoting these Relocate to Tax-Free Florida seminars.

If you decide to become a resident of another state to avoid inheritance taxes, take the time and spend the money to get professional advice to do it correctly. This is a tax issue so hire a CPA and/or attorney as opposed to relying on people trying to get your business by scaring you with horror stories about heavily armed state tax officials who will put a lien on your grandchildren if you do not pay inheritance taxes to them.

A minority of states still impose inheritance taxes in order to encourage their wealthy senior citizens to move to other states which do not have death taxes. Other states like Florida, seek to attract wealthy seniors by eliminating their inheritance tax. Florida has even included a ban on inheritance taxes in their State Constitution to make it harder for state legislators to change the law.

CHAPTER SUMMARY

Single individuals with estates under $11,700,000 currently should not owe a federal estate tax. Married couples have an unlimited marital deduction and can transfer to children and grandchildren up to $23,400,000 through portability. Some states impose estate and inheritance taxes at far lower levels. Income taxes on gains might be avoided when estate assets receive a stepped-up cost basis when an asset owner dies. The cost basis of inherited assets takes on the value as of the date of death which could eliminate income taxes on the gains when sold.

TAKE ACTION

- Review your estate planning documents if they were drafted several years ago when federal estate taxes were imposed at much lower levels. Consult with an estate planning attorney to make sure you are taking advantage of the ability to transfer

$11,700,000 plus to your children or grandchildren if you are not leaving all your assets to a surviving spouse.

- Structure your assets to take advantage of a stepped-up cost basis when you die. Having assets in the right type of accounts enables your heirs to inherit appreciated assets without having to pay income taxes on the gains.
- If you live in one of the 12 states that tax estates or in one of the six states that tax inheritances, hire a CPA to calculate how much you would owe your home state when you died tomorrow. Decide if the amount you might owe is worth the disruption of moving to a state with no or lower transfer taxes.

Section Two: Control Your Debt

Chapter 13 – Credit Cards

"There is scarcely anything that drags a person down like debt.'
P.T. Barnum

CONTROL YOUR DEBT

Section Two on how to EMPLOY wealth covers the need to CONTROL YOUR DEBT so that the money you have is working harder for you and is not being wasted on excessive finance charges. Types of debt that are discussed in this Section are: 1) Credit card debt; 2) Student loan debt; and 3) Debt to buy a house.

To GET wealth, the goal is not to eliminate debt but to use it wisely. Let debt work for you by making debt your employee, not your boss.

Start by reviewing your credit score and report to find out how agencies view your credit worthiness and what accounts are listed. Federal law gives you the right to obtain a free credit report every 12 months from the three major credit scoring companies: Experian, Equifax and Transunion. Call (877) 322-8228 or go to www.annualcreditreport.com to order your free reports. Make sure you are not being redirected to a fee-based service. Order these free reports every 12 months to monitor your progress as you work to better control your debts.

CHAPTER PREVIEW

Credit card debt is the first type of debt you need to control.

Americans love their credit cards. Why not? Credit cards reduce the need for carrying cash, they provide a record of your financial transactions, and they frequently provide cash rebates or benefits like travel miles which enable you to fly somewhere and spend even more money with your credit cards.

The problem with credit cards is obviously not how easy they are to use but that it can be very expensive to pay off your account balance. Rarely is the saying: "There is no such thing as a free lunch" more accurate than with credit cards. Every time your credit card is used, you should treat that purchase the same way you would if you were handing over your hard-earned cash rather than a piece of plastic.

Unlike cash which charges you no fee to use it, credit cards are loaded with fees to cover the convenience of their use. Regardless of what you read in the many mailings credit card issuers send out or the massive number of commercials you see, credit card use is not free.

Despite the huge increase in unemployment caused by COVID 19, credit card offers are still flooding consumers. As reported in The Wall Street Journal of 9/21/2020, according to Mintel, a research firm, 99 million credit card offers were mailed to individuals in July 2020. Just one month before, in June 2020, 57 million offers had been mailed. While the effort to support the U.S. Post Office is appreciated, the offers are going out because the business is so profitable to the credit card issuers.

In this chapter, the following aspects of credit card debt will be discussed:
- Credit card traps
- Paying off credit card debt
- Avoiding future credit card debt

1. CREDIT CARD TRAPS

There is nothing inherently wrong with using credit cards. The problem is that many people fail to understand the financial quicksand they could be walking into every time they charge something on their credit cards.

Fees imposed by credit cards include loan shark interest rates, annual fees and merchant fees.

Loan Shark Interest Rates

Do you use your credit card for convenience or because you do not currently have the money to pay cash for what you are buying?

If you are confident that you will be able to pay off the credit card balance on your next monthly statement, you are using your card for convenience. It is easier and safer to shop and dine with a piece of plastic than a wad of green papers with images out of your sixth-grade American history book.

On the other hand, if you know you cannot afford to pay off the balance on your next statement, then every time you use your credit card, you are putting yourself in additional high-interest debt. How high depends on the credit card and your current credit rating. But realize that when you carry a balance on your credit card, you are helping to finance the credit card company ads on television, the internet, in mailings to consumers, etc. What's in your wallet? A credit card loading you up on debt?

EXAMPLE 1: Vince recently received an offer from a credit card issuer to transfer balances from another card and pay zero percent interest for 12 months on the transferred debt. Since Vince was paying an interest rate of 12%, he transfers the balance from his current card to the new card. Unfortunately, instead of paying down the balance with the money he was spending on interest, Vince continues to use his old credit card and makes minimum payments on the new card. At the end of the 12-month introductory period, the interest rate on the new card goes up to 15% and Vince has an even deeper credit hole than before.

Federal law now requires credit card companies to disclose to you how many years it will take for you to pay off the debt at the rate you are paying. Since it is likely that you are continuing to use your credit card and therefore the debt keeps increasing, your debt will keep growing until the credit card company caps your credit card limit.

If you make only minimum payments on your credit card debt, check your statement and see how long it is projected that you will be paying on that debt. Make sure you are sitting down. Was that meal, trip, concert, clothing, etc. really worth 10 years of payments?

Annual Use Fees

In addition to charging high interest rates on outstanding debt, credit card companies frequently impose an annual fee for the privilege of charging you high interest rates on your unpaid balance. What a deal. These fees can range from $25 per year to several hundred dollars to access cards with major "perks." Do you know if any of your credit cards charge you an annual fee? If yes, how much is the fee and what are you getting for the fee? Membership fees only have value if the fees you pay get you something that you will use – like cash.

Credit cards which provide you with airline miles that expire in one year are of no benefit to you if you are unlikely to travel within the next 12 months due to COVID restrictions. Consider switching from a high annual fee credit card to a free card with the same company while you are unable or unwilling to travel. In most cases, your accumulated miles are not cancelled. When airplane travel again becomes more likely, then switch back to the annual fee card.

Airline mileage, cash rebates, etc. obviously cost the credit card issuers money. Make sure you are not the user paying for those free benefits with an interest rate that even Louie's EZ Loan Shop cannot get people to pay.

Merchant Fees

You use your charge card, the stores, restaurants, airlines, etc. have to pay a fee to Mastercard, Visa, PayPal, American Express, etc. for those companies to process your credit card transaction. This is why you will sometimes see gas stations advertising a lower price per gallon for cash payments.

Do the math before you pay extra to use your credit card. Incurring a five percent (5%) service fee to pay your property taxes with a credit card just to get a one percent (1%) cash rebate is obviously not wise money management.

While you cannot control merchant fees (other than not using your credit card), you can control the interest you pay. Either only charge if you can pay off the entire balance on your next monthly credit card statement or know that you should be able to pay off all your balances within three months. Longer than that and you own one of the expensive commercials promoting what is in your wallet.

2. PAYING OFF CREDIT CARD DEBT

"If you find yourself in a hole, stop digging."
Will Rogers

Approximately 55% of Americans do not pay off their credit card debt every month. Sometimes this cannot be avoided since you had to use your credit card for a large purchase like an appliance that stopped working and could not be repaired. But what about those non-essential expenses that you charge every month? Given the extremely high interest rates you incur on unpaid credit card debt, you really are digging the hole faster if you are not paying off your statement balances every month as they come in.

Some people try to manage their debt by taking advantage of credit cards which offer an introductory interest rate that is very attractive, sometimes even zero for short periods of time. Moving your credit card debt to a new card with a lower rate only works if you force yourself to pay off the debt before the low interest grace period on the new card expires. Plus, these great offers frequently require that you pay a fee up-front to take advantage of the deal. To reduce a credit card balance costing you 12%, paying a 3% fee to get a zero percent rate works if you pay off the new card balance before the rate shoots up.

Again, there is no free lunch at Le Credit Card Café. Credit card companies know that a majority of the people taking advantage of zero interest or low interest promotions are very likely to still have balances on their card when the interest rate goes from zero to 15%.

Effective ways to pay off credit card debt include: 1) Attacking the highest interest rate cards; 2) Obtaining a cash collateral loan; and 3) Borrowing from your retirement plan.

Attack High Interest Rate Cards

If you have multiple illnesses, you will logically focus on trying to treat the one that is most threatening to your health. Treat your credit card debt the same way. Attack those credit card balances which have you paying the highest interest rates because those are most threatening to your financial health. Should a doctor treat your sprained ankle or your heart attack first?

In the event you have multiple credit cards with unpaid balances, start by listing all your credits, the current unpaid balance, the interest rate you are now paying and the telephone number for their customer service. Yes, this means that you will actually have to do those statements you get every month. Check every statement to see how many years it will take to pay off that balance based on making only minimum payments. Now you see why credit card companies can advertise so much.

Start with the card charging the highest rate of interest. Try to pay at least twice the minimum payment. It may not seem like you are making progress, but you are. Go to the next card on the list and again make a double payment as many times as you can.

Always send something, even if it is only the minimum payment. Otherwise, the credit card companies could increase the already high interest payment you are not paying because you are deemed to be high risk. One could argue that this makes as much sense as pouring gasoline on a fire that a person was unable to put out with water, but it happens.

After making at least double the minimum payment for two months, call the credit card company and ask if the interest rate you are being charged could be lowered. Explain that you are trying to get a better handle on your debt, and you would greatly appreciate any rate reduction that you might be entitled to. Be polite. It is highly unlikely that the customer service person you are speaking with owns the company. You may get a slightly lower rate which means more money is going towards your debt.

Even if you are not successful in getting a rate reduction, keep trying. As you pay down debt, you are making yourself a more attractive card holder. How you are treated will help you determine which credit card companies you want to deal with once your debt is eliminated and your credit score is improved making you an attractive client.

Cash Collateral Loans

In addition to paying down your highest interest rates first, another option is to replace your high-cost debt with a longer maturity debt at a lower interest rate. A cash collateral loan might be an option for you if you are lucky enough to have someone, usually a family member, willing to help you.

When you have a lot of credit card debt, your credit score is usually going to make you far less attractive to lenders who offer lower rate personal loans. Instead of asking a parent or other relative to loan you money to pay off your credit card debt (again), instead ask if they would be willing to help you get a cash collateral loan.

A person with cash invests in a CD or savings account at a bank or a credit union which offers cash secured loans. The account owner agrees to allow their CD or account to be used as collateral to secure a loan. The borrower applies for a loan based on the maturity date of the CD. Since the loan will be backed by "cash" held at the bank or credit union, there is little risk for the financial institution to make the loan and even people with poor credit are frequently approved.

In addition to getting a loan which might otherwise never be approved before because of the borrower's poor credit, the interest rate on a cash collateral loan is usually based on the interest rate being paid to the CD or account owner so the rate paid by the borrower is substantially lower than an unsecured personal loan. Some credit unions and banks will charge two percent more on the loan than what they are paying on the CD or savings account. If the CD is earning two percent (2%) per year for five years, the cash collateral loan could be made at four percent (4%) for the same five period. See EXAMPLE 2 below.

Math quiz time: Which is more expensive to the borrower? Twelve percent (12%) paid to the credit card company or four percent (4%) paid to the credit union or bank which made the cash collateral loan? Plus, the CD or account owner continues to receive two percent (2%) as long as the borrower continues to make loan payments.

EXAMPLE 2: Eric paying fifteen percent (15%) on $20,000 of credit card debt which he took on while attending grad school. Eric's retired parents have given him money in the past to cover monthly bills, but the debt keeps growing and Eric's credit score is continuing to decline. Instead of just sending Eric a check, they enable Eric to obtain a cash collateral loan to pay off the credit cards. Eric's parents invest $20,000 in a five-year CD paying them two percent (2%) per year and agree to let Eric use the CD to secure a loan. Eric applies for and obtains a five-year cash collateral loan for $20,000 at an annual interest rate of four percent (4%) from the credit union. Eric uses the $20,000 to pay off his credit card debt and makes all the payments to pay off the loan in five years, Eric's parents receive two percent (2%) per year on the CD and the $20,000 is paid back to them at maturity.

There is risk involved for the owner of the CD or account being used as collateral. If the borrower fails to make payments on their loan, the credit union or bank are permitted to take the payments from the owner's account. This is why the cash collateral loans are attractive to the lender. They do not have to chase someone to reclaim a car moved to another state or take an unemployed person to court.

Most financial institutions doing cash collateral loans will base the loan interest rate on a percentage over what they are paying on the CD. In one case, the credit union charged a two percent fee, so the grandson got the used car loan at 6% for five years (4% paid on the CD plus 2% fee). Given the grandson's credit score and the normal rate on used car loans, this was a real deal.

In addition to paying down credit card debt, cash collateral loans can be used to secure loans to buy used cars, provide down payments for homes and to enable family members who are starting new businesses to get loans and a credit record so they can eventually borrow without pledging cash.

Make sure you check with several banks and credit unions when considering cash collateral loans. Some institutions charge a flat interest, regardless of the interest rate they are paying on the cash being used as collateral. Be careful with using floating rate investment accounts since the interest rate will probably float as well. I prefer using a fixed rate CD as collateral so that the loan interest is fixed as well. This also enables the term of the loan to match the term of the CD.

Borrow From Your Retirement Plan

Rarely should you borrow from your retirement plan at work. Too many people take advantage of loans from their 401(k) or 403(b) plans to cover non-essential items (like cosmetic surgery).

But if you are paying 15% interest on a credit card balance that keeps growing, how are you coming out ahead by having funds in a retirement account that will have to be used to help pay off the credit card balance? If you cannot pay off your credit card balance when you are working, what is the likelihood you will be able to pay it off when you are retired?

3. AVOIDING FUTURE CREDIT CARD DEBT

The best way to avoid falling off a cliff is to not go near one. Use your credit cards for convenience and safety (not having to carry cash) rather than treating them as free money.

COVID-19 Impact On Credit Card Debt

Restrictions on dining out, traveling and entertainment have substantially reduced new credit card debt. As reported in The Wall Street Journal on 8/3/2020: "In the U.S., total outstanding credit card debt fell by 11%, or $100 billion, between February and the end of

June, according to Equifax. April was the largest monthly drop in revolving credit on record, while May was the second largest."

The Wall Street Journal article attributes the reduction in debt to temporary government action: "The combination of state and federal unemployment benefits has meant that around two-thirds of U.S. workers who were laid off or furloughed are eligible to receive more in unemployment than they were earning on the job, according to a study by economists at the University of Chicago. The U.S. stimulus legislation also allowed people to defer payments on their federally backed mortgages for up to a year and most federal student loans through September. Those measures have given many people who were living for years with large credit card debt balances extra funds to pay them down."

While this reduction in credit card debt is certainly good news, it is likely to be reversed very quickly once people are allowed to resume their spending habits. So now is an excellent time to control your credit card debt by paying down your current debt and adopting better ways to utilize your cards.

Credit Card Use Rules

Rule #1: Try never to use a credit card if you cannot pay off the entire balance when the next monthly bill arrives. The interest rate charged by banks on outstanding balances makes loan sharking look reasonable. Rule #2: If you have to use a credit card and know you will not be able to pay off your balance when the statement arrives, then force yourself to use your card as little as possible in the upcoming months until the balance is zero. Rule #3: Try to limit the use of your credit cards to circumstances like making travel reservations or cases where you do not want to be carrying more cash than you are comfortable having in your procession.

CHAPTER SUMMARY

Credit cards provide great convenience but at the price of high interest rates on unpaid balances and high annual fees on cards that offer the most benefits. The interest charges on outstanding debt are so high that they can easily cause unsuspecting card users to have to declare bankruptcy. You need to restrict your use of credit cards to have any hope of achieving financial independence.

TAKE ACTION

- Pay off and cancel your high annual fee and high interest rate credit cards.
- Consider obtaining a cash collateral loan to pay off high interest credit card balances.
- Limit your credit card purchases to an amount you know you can pay off every month.

Chapter 14 – College Loans

"Money often costs too much."
Ralph Waldo Emerson

CHAPTER PREVIEW

Student loans are a second source of debt you need to control as you EMPLOY your wealth.

The cost of higher education is creating huge new classes of people burdened with student loan debt. According to an article dated 2/3/2020 on Forbes.com, "The latest student loan debt statistics for 2020 show how serious the student loan debt crisis has become for borrowers across all demographics and age groups. There are 45 million borrowers who collectively owe $1.6 trillion in student loan debt in the U.S. The average student loan debt for members of the Class of 2018 is $29,200, a 2% increase from the prior year, according to the Institute for College Access and Success."

Only mortgage debt (Chapter 15) is higher than the total amount of student loan debt in the U.S.

In Chapter 2 (Tax-Favored Assets), we recommended utilizing 529 plans to save for college. But if you were unable to save enough to cover the cost of college for yourself, your children or grandchildren, do not waste time and energy beating yourself up. Recall the saying: "When you are up to your neck in alligators, it is hard to remember that your initial objective was to drain the swamp."

In this chapter, three aspects of paying for higher education will be discussed:

- Lower cost college options
- Student financial aid
- Restructuring debt

To cover the gap between what you have saved and what you may need, focus your efforts on finding lower-cost education options.

Apply for whatever financial assistance might you qualify for and if you have to take out loans, manage them by making sure you are paying the lowest possible interest rate for the shortest length of time.

1. LOWER COST COLLEGE OPTIONS

"If you don't know where you are going,
you might wind up someplace else."
Yogi Berra

Nearly half of all student loan borrowers in the U.S. wish they had selected a cheaper college according to the Financial Industry Regulatory Authority's Invest Education Foundation. You would hopefully never buy a car that you knew in advance you could not afford. Taking on student debt to attend an expensive college without the likelihood of getting a decent job to pay back the debt is to doom yourself to decades of financial frustration.

Are you going to college to prepare for a particular career or to try and find one? If you are undecided on a career, you are not alone. Many college students will change their declared major multiple times before they graduate. But those classes in your rejected major(s) are expensive and time-consuming. You will avoid a lot of student loan debt by researching your education options prior to loading up your car and heading for that beautiful tree-filled campus anchored by fortress-like buildings built with more stone than was carved on Mount Rushmore.

There are a lot of free resources available to help you investigate college options. One excellent source of information is the website: studentaid.gov operated by the U.S. Department of Education. In addition to providing information about student aid, the website also can help you decide which colleges and universities might be a better fit for you.

Community Colleges

Before you take on a huge amount of debt to attend the college your mother and father attended or your boyfriend or girlfriend is going to, ask yourself: What career am I preparing for at college?

Most Bachelor of Arts (B.A.) and Bachelor of Science (B.S.) degrees require a substantial number of introductory classes taught in lecture halls that hold more sleeping students than a college dorm at 10:00 a.m. on a Sunday morning after a night football game. Since the first two years of a traditional four-year degree program are frequently spent taking introductory classes, why not take those classes at a reduced rate at a community college and transfer the credits when you move to the institution offering the B.A. or B.S. degree?

There are now 10,000 community colleges in the U.S. Since they receive funds from both state and local taxes, the cost of attending a community college is substantially less than a university. Especially with more college classes being taught on-line, consider getting those introductory credits at the lowest cost per credit hour at your local community college.

In-State Colleges

Over the past several years, state legislatures have been substantially decreasing the amount of financial assistance they have been providing public colleges and universities. Even with reduced funding from state legislatures, attending a college or university within your state is usually a better option than going out of state. For proof, compare the tuition cost for an in-state student vs one from another state or country.

If you have already decided you intend to pursue a particular career and you can only get the appropriate degree from a particular school that is in a different state, try to take as many introductory classes as possible at your local community college or in-state school and then transfer to complete the major.

For Profit College Alert

Education has been discovered by big business to be a profit center. For-profit colleges have become extremely good at attracting students who need to borrow to finance their education and are likely to be approved for loans. The result is that students attending for profit schools have a higher loan default rate because they are less successful at obtaining well-paying jobs in their chosen field.

According to a report by the Federal Reserve that was last updated on 1/30/2020: "Repayment status also differs by the type of institution attended. Over one-fifth of borrowers who attended private for-profit institutions are behind on student loan payments, versus 8 percent who attended public institutions and 5 percent who attended private not-for-profit institutions."

While not all for-profit schools should automatically be rejected, when trying to control the cost of student debt, the less you have to borrow, the more funds you have available to build your wealth. Give very serious consideration to attending your local community college and an in-state school before you enroll in a school located in another state or a for-profit school.

2. STUDENT FINANCIAL AID

One of the best ways to keep your student debt manageable is to take maximum advantage of scholarships, Federal Pell grants, Stafford loans and support programs that are available at most colleges and universities.

The starting point for individuals considering going to or having been accepted to college is to complete the Free Application for Federal Student Aid, or FAFSA. Granted it is an extensive application but remember you are asking for money, and you should show that you need it.

An excellent article appeared in the March 19, 2019, issue of The Wall Street Journal regarding the need to file the Free Application for Federal Student Aid.

The article stated: "The review of 2.4 million FAFSA submitted between Oct. 1, 2017, and Oct. 31, 2018, for aid that would cover the

2018-19 academic year, found that 30% of students whose parents' adjusted gross income was in the lowest quintile submitted their FAFSA after March 1, 2018. Meanwhile, two-thirds of those whose parents were in the highest income quintile, earning upward of $133,000, submitted it by Feb. 1."

Why is early filing of the FAFSA important? Because several states award funds on a first come basis. If you file late or just later, the limit pool of available money might already be allocated.

Another article in The Wall Street Journal of January 6, 2020, listed the following free search engines to try and obtain scholarships:

> Careeronestop.org
> Cappex.com
> Collegeboard.com
> Fastweb.com
> Goingmerry.com
> Scholarshipamerica.org
> Scolarships.com
> Scholarsnapp.org
> Studentscholarshipseach.com
> Unigo.com

Do not get discouraged if initial results do not produce that full ride you would love to have. As hockey great Wayne Gretzky once said: "You miss 100% of the shots you don't take."

3. LOAN RESTRUCTURING

Many individuals have so much student debt that they are in default. Banks holding the debt have decided that it would be better to take a lower interest rate than to have to accept default. What may have been a loan for 10 years at 5% is restructured into a 15-year loan at 6 percent. While that payment might be the same, the amount of interest paid will be substantially more.

Some lenders have developed companies which focus on refinancing student loans. One such company is Student Loan Hero which is a division of Lending Tree. While we are not endorsing them, their website at studentloanhero.com is one source of information that is worth checking.

Loan forgiveness programs

Your student loans could be cancelled if you decide to participate in a loan forgiveness program. Basically, you agree to provide services like teaching in a low-income community for 10 years. There are additional requirements like continuing to make regular payments on your loans during your service period. A list of some of these programs can be found at studentloanhero.com. Regardless of which program looks attractive to you, make sure you understand all the requirements that have to be met in order to receive loans forgiveness.

One popular federal program is Public Service Loan Forgiveness (PSLF). To qualify for loan forgiveness, you must work 10 years for certain institutions that are non-profits or for an organization like AmeriCorps. Not all nonprofits qualify and not all student loans are eligible to be forgiven.

What if you teach in a financially deprived area for 10 years, will your debt be cancelled? Unfortunately, there have been lawsuits saying that people have fulfilled their 10-year obligation but have found that there are some other requirements that they were not aware of.

Instead of restructuring a loan, some borrowers feel that their loans should be forgiven. There are a variety of reasons given for their proposal including that excessive student loans are causing people to delay starting families and buying homes. But the taxpayers who are being asked to fund the loan payoffs frequently paid for their own college education.

Instead of just cancelling student loans with taxpayer contributions, a better approach would be to use the borrowing power of the United States government to back a refinancing effort. Why not issue 20-year U.S. savings bonds which pay tax free income at maturity? Cap the amount of education savings bonds that can be purchased at $20,000 per year, $100,000 total per person. Unlike Roth IRAs, eliminate income caps to encourage high-income taxpayers to purchase them. Use the bond sale proceeds to create a pool of funds to refinance student loans. It worked in World War II to help finance the war effort. Why not a similar effort to attack this huge debt problem?

CHAPTER SUMMARY

Community colleges and in-state schools can substantially reduce the cost of obtaining a college degree. Once you reduce your potential tuition costs as low as possible, aggressively pursue financial aid. Only after you have exhausted other options, apply for the student loans. Even after being approved, constantly check to see if there is a lower interest rate available for refinancing your loans. Interest rates and terms can change so do not check once and live with your loan until paid off years later.

TAKE ACTION

- Especially if you are undecided on your future career path, enroll at your local community college to take the core classes that are required for graduation at both the community college and most universities. Take the opportunity at the community college to explore associate degree programs to help identify possible career paths at a much-reduced cost.
- Treat pursuing student aid and scholarships like a job. The potential payouts could greatly exceed the money you make per hour working. There is money available to help you attend college. But you have to work to find these funds. Nobody is coming to hand them to you.
- After you apply for student loans, do not treat them as cast in stone. Control your debt by frequently checking to see if there is a lower interest available that you can take advantage of by restructuring your loan.

Chapter 15 – Buying a Home

"Real estate cannot be lost or stolen, nor can it be carried away. Purchased with common sense, paid for in full, and managed with reasonable care, it is about the safest investment in the world."
Franklin D. Roosevelt

CHAPTER PREVIEW

Financing the purchase of a home is a third major source of debt you need to control to more effectively EMPLOY your wealth.

The largest single debt that most people take on is usually a mortgage to purchase a home. For many, the "American Dream" is to have a house where they are building value, or equity.

Home ownership is admittedly not for everyone. You might be a recent college graduate who is anxious to acquire different work experiences and is willing to frequently switch jobs and locations. Having a house ties you down to a particular location at a time when you are not sure where you want to establish yourself. In that case renting makes more sense.

However, home ownership is still a major goal for most people. They do not want to pay rent to a landlord forever. When you own a home, you have control over your purchase, within the regulations of your community. When you rent, you can move much easier, but you have little control over your apartment or rental house.

If you decide to become a homeowner, whether it be a single-family residence, condo or co-op, you will probably use a mortgage or land contract to finance the purchase.

In this chapter, we address the following subjects concerning buying a home:
- Home ownership in America
- Types of mortgages
- Land contracts vs mortgages

1. HOME OWNERSHIP IN AMERICA

The U.S. Home Ownership Rate is the percentage of homes in the United States which are occupied by the owner(s). While the Home Ownership Rate in the U.S. has been declining, low interest rates are making mortgages more affordable which could reverse this trend. Offsetting lower interest rates, however, is the steep demand for housing that has resulted in multiple bids for houses, increasing the cost of housing.

The United States Census Bureau reported on February 2, 2021, "The homeownership rate of 65.8 percent was 0.7 percentage points higher than the rate in the fourth quarter 2019 (65.1 percent) and 1.6 percent lower than the rate in the third quarter 2020 (67.4 percent)."

According to an article in The Wall Street Journal of 6/1/2020: "Younger generations have been buying homes at lower rates than their predecessors. While the overall homeownership rate in the U.S. last year was more than 64%, less than 37%, of people under the age of 35 owned homes, according to the U.S. Census Bureau. That is down from highs of nearly 44% and an average of 39% for that age group over the past three decades."

A 6/10/2020 article on Zillow.com stated: "More than 32 million adults lived with a parent or grandparent as of April, according to a Zillow analysis of Current Population Survey data up 9.7% from the same period a year ago and the highest level on record."

These moves are not solely related to COVID 19 layoffs and closed colleges. Again, from the 6/10/2020 article on Zillow.com: "It is not just newly jobless young Americans that are moving back home. Before the pandemic, almost half (46.5%) of employed young adults already lived in a parent's home; by April (2020), the share had risen to 49%. Those who ceased looking for work altogether or were not in the labor force already, including a large number of students, were even more likely to move back home, adding another million plus young adults to the ranks of homeward-bound movers."

Hopefully soon, COVID 19 will be controlled, and people will be able to resume working with more certainty that their jobs will be secure. When people feel more economically secure, they will be far more likely to be looking to purchase homes. As much as your parents might appreciate having someone on site to cut their grass, they would be happy if you had your own place to live,

EXAMPLE 1: Mary and Eric recently got married and hope to start a family soon. They both anticipate not having to travel as much for their jobs and feel relatively confident that they will be able to continue to work at their current employers for the foreseeable future. Both Mary and Eric have rented apartments in different states and want to start building equity in a house. While Eric still has $40,000 of student loans to pay off, they check with a local bank which pre-qualifies them to borrow up to $200,000. Historically low interest rates make the potential monthly payment affordable. Using a real estate agent, they view several houses and ultimately purchase a small starter home.

Decide if you are ready and able to become a homeowner. Ask yourself: Is your current job secure? Do you like the area where you currently live? Are there houses you can afford in areas where you might want to live? If you decide to relocate to another area too far away to commute to, is it likely that you will be able to sell your home within a reasonable period of time for close to what you paid for it? The more yes answers you give to the previous questions, the more likely you will be successful in finding and purchasing a home.

2. TYPES OF MORTGAGES

Buying a house in America is not a cheap project. The U.S. Census Bureau reported, "In the fourth quarter 2020, the median asking sales price for vacant for sale units was $214,600." Although some individuals are able to pay cash for a home, the majority of potential buyers finance the purchase of a home with a mortgage or land contract.

Once you decide to buy a house and apply for a mortgage, how long do you want the term of the loan? Although most mortgages are made for either 15 or 30 years, it is not unusual to have mortgages for terms of 10 or 20 years. The monthly payment you can afford is the frequent driver of the type of the mortgage you will qualify for. The following Table A compares financing the purchase of a house using either a 15-year or a 30-year mortgage.

Table A

Home Price	$200,000	
Down payment	$40,000 (20% of purchase price)	
Interest rate	3.8%	
Monthly payment	15 year $1,450.85	30 year $1,028.87
Interest paid over term	15 year $50,155.19	30 year $108,391.43

Table A above shows that while the monthly payment of $1,450.85 for the 15-year mortgage is substantially higher than the monthly payment of $1,028.87 for the 30-year mortgage, the interest that will be paid on the 30-year loan is much higher. While reducing the interest you pay is important, you have to be able to comfortably afford the monthly payment.

EXAMPLE 2: John and Ann are married and are purchasing what they hope will be their last home. Both John and Ann are working and plan to retire in approximately 15 years. They want to have their house paid off prior to retiring so they apply for a 15-year mortgage. While the monthly payment will be higher for a 15-year mortgage compared to a 30-year mortgage, they can afford the higher monthly payment and want the peace of mind in retirement of knowing their house is paid for.

Not everyone plans to stay for many years in the house they are buying. You may know that you might have to move to change jobs. Or the housing market where you are considering buying is hot and you hope to buy a house, make improvements while living there and then sell it hopefully at a nice profit and move up to a larger, more expensive home. In those cases, the lower monthly payments of a 30-

year mortgage might make more sense even if the interest paid is higher.

EXAMPLE 3: Alex is single and is looking to buy his first home. Although Alex has a good job, he still has tens of thousands of dollars of student loans outstanding, so he wants to keep his mortgage payment as low as possible. Alex decides to obtain a 30-year fixed-rate mortgage. While the monthly payment will be lower since he is paying back the amount borrowed over 30 years, the amount Alex will pay on principal will be extremely low.

If you do not have funds available to put 20% down, then explore options other than a conventional mortgage. There are federal and state programs that encourage home buying substantially reducing the amount of a down payment. If you are a veteran, these options can be extremely helpful.

Mortgage Insurance

When you do not have 20% to put down, lenders will usually require that you purchase mortgage insurance. Like any type of insurance, this will require that you pay an insurance premium. While it could be well-worth the added cost to begin building equity in a house, make sure that once you own over 20% of the value of the house, you request that the mortgage insurance be cancelled. Why continue to pay for insurance that is no longer required?

3. LAND CONTRACTS

Land contracts are alternatives to mortgages. Instead of obtaining a mortgage through a bank, credit union or mortgage broker, the seller(s) of the property provide the means for the buyer to finance the purchase.

Land contracts are usually more popular when interest rates are higher. Potential buyers might not qualify for a mortgage if interest rates make the monthly payments too high for the buyers to handle.

From a legal standpoint, a land contract is an agreement between potential buyers wanting to purchase a house or piece of real estate and the owners of the target property who are interested in selling.

After a purchase agreement is signed by the buyers and sellers, a land contract is prepared which contains the financing terms for the purchase. In land contracts, the sellers take the place of a bank or mortgage company providing the funds to complete the sale.

Just as the company or individual holding a mortgage assumes the risk that the buyers will default by not making payments, the holder of a land contract also assumes the same default risk.

EXAMPLE 4: John wants to buy a condo for $150,000. Because John owes $70,000 on college loans, he has been told by several banks and credit unions that he will not qualify for a mortgage. The seller of the condo believes John's job prospects are excellent and agrees to sell him the condo by having John sign a land contract. The seller is retired and likes that the land contract will pay him a higher rate of interest than he can currently get at a bank or credit union. John makes a down payment of 10% ($15,000) and signs a land contract for $135,000 ($150,000 sales price minus $15,000 down payment equals $135,000).

When someone is buying a house using a land contract, they do not obtain title until the land contract is paid off. If you are buying a house using a land contract, consider having a title company hold the title until the house is paid off. Otherwise, several years later after paying off the land contract, you have to make sure the sellers of the house are still able to execute a deed transferring the property to you.

If a buyer defaults on a land contract, the buyer loses the funds that have been paid to the holder of the land contract.

CHAPTER SUMMARY

Homeownership is encouraged in the United States through income tax incentives that are not available to people who rent. Mortgages vary in length (10, 15, 20 or 30 years) and in terms (fixed rate or variable). Generally, longer term mortgages require smaller monthly payments but result in more loan interest being paid. Land contracts can be used to purchase a house when getting a mortgage is not an option, usually due to credit issues. They are less available when mortgage rates are low but can be used when a potential buyer's credit score is not high due to college debt or other financial problems.

TAKE ACTION

- Decide if you are ready to buy a house. If your job is secure and you anticipate staying in a particular location for at least two years, start looking for houses on-line and narrow your options before contacting a real estate agent.
- Consider how much you can afford to pay per month for a house payment. Compare the costs of using a 10, 15, 20 or 30-year mortgage to purchase a house.
- If you do not qualify to obtain an affordable mortgage, consider purchasing a house on a land contract. Not all sellers will accept land contracts so be prepared to have fewer potential houses to choose from

Section Three: Manage Your Retirement

Chapter 16 – Social Security

"The (Social Security) system is not intended as a substitute for private savings, pension plans, and insurance protection. It is, rather, intended as the foundation upon which these other forms of protection can be soundly built. Thus, the individual's own work, his planning and his thrift will bring him a higher standard of living upon his retirement, or his family a higher standard of living in the event of his death, than would otherwise be the case. Hence the system both encourages thrift and self-reliance and helps to prevent destitution in our national life."
Dwight D. Eisenhower

MANAGE YOUR RETIREMENT

Section Three on how to EMPLOY your wealth describes the need to MANAGE YOUR RETIREMENT like you would manage a business. Since the average American life expectancy is 78, if you retire at 65, you could spend 20 or more years in retirement. To effectively manage your wealth during those decades, you need to have a basic understanding of 1) Social Security; 2) Health care in retirement; and 3) Income distributions from retirement plans.

CHAPTER PREVIEW

Social Security is the first program you should learn to manage in retirement. The Social Security Act was passed in 1935 during the Great Depression. The goal of the Act was to provide all Americans some type of regular payment in retirement from a government administered program. Besides retirement payments, in 1956, "the

Social Security Act was amended to provide monthly benefits to permanently and totally disabled workers aged 50-64" according to the Social Security Administration (SSA).

Social Security is an extremely popular financial support program in America. In 2021, approximately 65 million Americans will receive a monthly social security benefit which means over one trillion will be paid out in benefits this year. Payments to 46 million retired workers will average $1,544 per month. An estimated 8.2 million disabled workers will be paid $10.5 billion in monthly payments averaging $1,258. Retired workers and their dependents receive 73.2% of all benefits paid. Disabled workers and their dependents receive 14.5% of benefits paid.

As reported by the Social Security Administration (SSA), "Nearly nine out of ten individuals aged 65 and older receive Social Security benefits" which "… represent about 33% of the income of the elderly."

These payments are critical for a majority of people over 65. Again, according to the Social Security Administration: "Among elderly Social Security beneficiaries, 50% of married couples and 70% of unmarried persons receive 50% or more of their income from Social Security. Among elderly Social Security beneficiaries, 21% of married couples and about 45% of unmarried persons relay on Social Security for 90% or more of their income."

Since an estimated 179 million workers are currently covered by Social Security, the program is not going away but will be different in the future. You need to understand how Social Security operates to maximize the benefits you have earned and are entitled to receive.

In this chapter, we will address the following aspects of Social Security:
- Funding Social Security
- Social Security retirement benefits
- Social Security family benefits

1. FUNDING SOCIAL SECURITY

When discussing Social Security, the question that comes up most frequently is if Social Security will even be available in the future. You need to know how Social Security is funded and how likely it is that the funding sources are secure.

Social Security Revenue

Social Security is funded by a 12.4 % payroll tax that is split evenly between employers and employees. If you are self-employed, you pay the entire 12.4 %. The Social Security tax is paid on earned income up to a cap of $137,700 in 2020.

In addition to paying into Social Security, Medicare, which covers hospital costs for individuals over 65, is funded by an additional 2.90 % tax, again split evenly between employers and employees.

Is Social Security Running Out of Money?

Although politicians do not want to admit it, Social Security is running out of money. As reported in the Bloomberg Businessweek issue of 8/31/2020: 'The (Social Security Administration) trustees' report this spring predicted the main fund would run out of money in 2034 and the disability fund in 2065. The Covid-19 pandemic is likely to accelerate the depletion of the main fund by two or three years by reducing payroll tax receipts and pushing people into earlier retirement ..."

There are three major reasons why Social Security is running out of money: 1) Fewer workers are paying into the System; 2) People are receiving more benefits than they are paying for; and 3) The rate of return stinks on the funds invested to pay future Social Security benefits.

Fewer workers are now paying into the Social Security system

In 1934 when the Social Security Act was passed, there were far more people paying into the system than were receiving benefits. For every one person getting a Social Security check in 1935, there were nine people contributing. The Social Security Administration reported in 2020: "There are currently 2.8 workers for each Social Security beneficiary. By 2035, there will be 2.3 covered workers for each beneficiary."

People are receiving more benefits than they paid for

Once activated, Social Security retirement benefits are paid until a person dies so if people live longer, they will receive more from the SSA. In 1934, the average life expectancy of an American was 59 years. Due to a combination of better health care, less physically demanding jobs and access to more and better food, the average life expectancy is now 78 years. If people now live an average of 19 years longer than they did in 1934, then some Social Security beneficiaries could receive over 200 more monthly payments than Americans born in 1934.

The investment return on Social Security trust funds is not keeping up with anticipated needs. Money deposited into Social Security is held in the Social Security Trust Fund. By law, Trust Funds can only be invested in super safe Treasury Bonds issued by the United States Treasury. While super safe from default, the interest paid on these bonds in 2019 was 1.2% per year. Since the rate of inflation in 2019 was .6%, the investment return was a whopping .6%.

Although proposals to invest the Trust Funds more aggressively have been shot down, something has to be done to improve the system in order for Social Security to be there when the workers now paying into the system retire and justifiably expect to receive a benefit they paid for.

Taxing Social Security Benefits

While 37 states currently do not tax Social Security benefits, the IRS is not so generous. If you are a single taxpayer with income including Social Security that is between $25,000 and $34,000, then 50% of your Social Security will be taxed. This does not mean you will send 50% of your payments to the IRS but that you will include 50% of the total Social Security payments you received in your taxable income total that is used to calculate the tax you owe.

Recall what your tax bracket was from Chapter 10. According to the Social Security Administration (SSA) website: "If you file a federal tax return as an individual and your combined income is between $25,000 and $34,000, you may have to pay income tax on up to 50 percent of your benefits." If your combined income is "....more than $34,000, up to 85 percent of your benefits may be taxable."

Again, from the SSA website: "If you file a joint return, and you and your spouse have a combined income that is between $32,000 and $44,000, you may have to pay income tax on up to 50 percent of your benefits." If your combined income is "...more than $44,000, up to 85 percent of your benefits may be taxable."

EXAMPLE 1: Mary and George are married, retired and together have their combined income over $44,000. Their Social Security is taxed at 85%. Mary and George are in the 12% tax bracket so 85% of their Social Security payments are taxed at 12 cents per dollar.

If you are considering moving after you retire, be sure to check out which of your target states tax Social Security and pensions. While lower state taxes should not be the only consideration to consider when moving, if you are going to be on a fixed income, this is important information to have which could impact your decision. Remember that state laws can change a lot faster than the weather.

Social Security Reforms

People running for political office love to talk about how they will "save" Social Security if and when they get elected. Once elected, however, politicians are shocked, shocked to find out that virtually all of the possible solutions to bailing out Social Security involve increasing taxes, something career politicians never do. Despite the TV commercials, there is no pot of gold at the end of the Lucky Charms rainbow. Politicians hope we will blame the leprechauns when Social Security benefits are cut approximately 75% as projected by the Social Security trustees this spring.

In addition to raising the payroll tax rate from the current 12.4%, Congress could increase the amount of income and wages subject to taxation from the current cap of $137,700 for 2020 which would result in a tax increase for higher wage earners. Congress could also shift funding Social Security from payroll taxes to general tax revenues which would capture income from higher income individuals but also add to our huge federal deficit.

2. SOCIAL SECURITY RETIREMENT BENEFITS

The Social Security Administration reports that 73.2% of all benefits paid are to retired workers. You need to know how benefits are calculated in order to effectively manage how you receive Social Security payments when you are retired.

Full Retirement Age

Social Security Full Retirement Age is how old you must be to qualify for 100% of your Social Security benefit. This is not your age when you retire. Full Retirement Age for the Social Security program depends on when you were born.

In an effort to safeguard Social Security for future generations of U.S. workers, Full Retirement Age is gradually going up to delay when participants can receive full benefits (TABLE A below). The later workers qualify for 100% of their Social Security benefit, the more money remains in the program to pay for future benefits.

Table A

Birth Year	Full Retirement Age
1943 - 1954	66
1955	66 and 2 months
1956	66 and 4 months
1957	66 and 6 months
1958	66 and 8 months
1959	66 and 10 months
1960 and after	67

In 2021, the maximum monthly Social Security retirement benefit is $3,148 for a person who waits until Full Retirement Age to start collecting. The average monthly payment is $1,543 for retirees.

Primary Insurance Amount (PIA)

Your Primary Insurance Amount (PIA) is the monthly amount you will receive at your Full Retirement Age (FRA). Your PIA is calculated on the average monthly earnings over the highest 35 years that you had earned income. Benefits are based on a percentage of your average monthly earnings but because PIA is capped, low-wage earners receive a higher percentage than high-wage workers.

Reduced Early Benefits

If you start taking benefits before your Full Retirement Age, your Social Security Benefits will be reduced for the rest of your life. The earliest you can claim retirement benefits is age 62. According to the Social Security Administration, in 2018, 31% of women and 27% of men activated their payments when they turned 62 even though it meant possibly receiving only 75% of their Full Retirement Age benefit. TABLE B shows the discounted amount you receive by activating your Social Security payments between 62 and 65.

Table B

Age Benefits Start	Percent of PIA
62	75%
63	80%
64	86%
65	93%

EXAMPLE 2: Fred was born in 1952. According to TABLE A above, his Full Retirement Age is 66. Fred decides to start taking Social Security benefits at age 62 instead of waiting. TABLE B above shows that Fred will receive 75% of the Social Security benefit he would have received his Full Retirement Age (FRA) of age 66. Other

than possible adjustments for inflation, Fred's benefit will be based on the reduced 75% amount for the rest of his life.

While some early filers claim they do not expect to live long enough to benefit from waiting for a higher amount, the life expectancy of someone who is 65 years old is approximately 20 years. Are you willing to accept a 25% pay cut in your benefits for an estimated 23 years in order to get Social Security early at age 62?

One other drawback to taking Social Security before Full Retirement Age is that if you earn over $18,960 per year in 2021, $1 of benefits will be held back for every $2 you earn over $18,960. If you are under Full Retirement Age, not only will you take a 25% benefit haircut for the rest of your life but 50% of your reduced benefit could be held back if you earn over $18,960 per year. You will eventually receive the 50% that was deducted back after you reach FRA, but it is paid overtime and could result in you paying higher income taxes. After you reach Full Retirement Age, there is no cap on the amount that you can earn and keep your entire monthly payment.

Increased Delayed Benefits

If you can afford to delay the start of taking your Social Security payments, your monthly benefit will increase for the rest of your life and possibly that of your spouse as well. Between your Full Retirement Age and age 70, your Social Security benefit that you postpone taking will increase eight percent (8%) per year to 132% of the amount you would receive at your FRA.

EXAMPLE 3: John was born in 1950 so his Full Retirement Age (FRA) is 66. John enjoys his current job and decides to delay taking Social Security. His benefit will increase eight percent (8%) per year until the year he turns 70. At that time, John's monthly benefit will be 132% of the amount he would have received at 66 and will go no higher so he activates his Social Security.

3. SOCIAL SECURITY FAMILY BENEFITS

Social Security benefits can be paid not only to a person's surviving spouse, but also to minor children of the deceased and even to a divorced spouse if certain conditions are met.

Spousal benefit

Spouses can claim up to 50% of their spouse's Primary Insurance Amount (PAI) if they have been married at least one year, are 62 or older and their spouse has filed to collect Social Security. This is an important benefit for spouses who may not have worked enough to qualify for their own benefit, they can receive up to 50% of their spouse's PAI if they have been married for at least one year and their spouse is receiving retirement or disability benefits.

Surviving spouse benefit

Surviving spouses can receive the benefit that their deceased spouse was getting if they were married for at least 9 months, the surviving spouse is 60 or older and the surviving spouse is unmarried when filing or remarried after turn 60.

EXAMPLE 4: Harry is 75 years old and is receiving the maximum Social Security benefit when he dies. Karen, his surviving spouse, is receiving a smaller benefit of $2,500 per month based on her part-time work. Since Harry has died, Karen can request Harry's benefit. She will not be able to receive two Social Security payments, so she logically accepts Harry's benefit.

Former spouse benefit

Many former spouses are surprised to learn that if you were married for at least 10 years before you became divorced, you might be able to collect a benefit based on your ex-spouse's record. To collect, you must be 62 or older, unmarried and your ex-spouse's benefit is larger than your PIA. It does not reduce the benefits of the ex-spouse.

Dependent children benefit

Dependent children and dependent grandchildren may be able to receive benefits based on your record. To qualify, the child must be unmarried, under age 18, under age 19 if they have not graduated from high school or over 18 and disabled from a disability that started before, they turned 22. Benefits paid to a child could impact their record. Be sure to make an appointment to discuss this option with a Social Security Administration representative before the child files for this benefit.

Dependent parent benefit

A parent who is receiving at least 50% of their support from a child who dies may be able to collect 82.5% of the Primary Insurance Amount of the deceased. Two dependent parents can each receive 50% of the PIA of the deceased child.

CHAPTER SUMMARY

Social Security is paid for payroll taxes which are split between employees and employers. Most Social Security payments are intended for income in retirement although SSA also pays for people who are permanently disabled. A surviving spouse and younger children of a person might be eligible to receive Social Security benefits upon the death of one spouse or parent.

TAKE ACTION

- Every year, verify that all your earnings for the previous year appear on your Social Security statement.
- Determine your Full Retirement Age and compare the monthly amounts you would receive early at age 62, at your Full Retirement Age and at age 70.
- Discuss with your spouse the benefit he or she would receive if you died first. Make sure they know where you keep your income tax records to help them file a claim.

Chapter 17 – Health Care

*"America's healthcare system is neither
healthy, caring, nor a system."*
Walter Cronkite

CHAPTER PREVIEW

*Health care is a second category you need to manage in retirement
as you EMPLOY your wealth more effectively.*

Health care in American is neither free nor easy to understand. Given your huge potential financial exposure if you have major health issues without adequate insurance, you need to take the time to learn what health care options you have before and after you retire. Many people unfortunately assume that once they are older, Medicare will automatically cover all their health care.

Medicare is not a one size fits all health care plan. Medicare has Parts A, B, C and D. Fortunately, there are multiple websites you can check which offer information about Medicare. There is also no shortage of individuals available who can provide recommendations about what are the best Medicare options for you. Be careful, however, since many of the so-called Medicare experts are salespeople paid to promote the products of the companies they represent. The more you understand about Medicare, the better you will be able to determine which Medicare plan and provider are right for you.

One of the most important reasons to save for retirement is to make sure you are able to afford health care coverage for yourself in retirement. Health care costs are the number one reason people cite for declaring personal bankruptcy.

Many people assume that all nursing home care is covered by Medicare. While custodial nursing home coverage might be available through other government programs like Medicaid and through the Veterans Administration, there are severe limits on the amount of assets and income you can have before you can receive the benefits.

Medicaid coverage is explained later in this chapter but realize that it is intended for people with minimal assets, in some cases requiring people to have less than $2,000 of liquid assets.

Health care in retirement is a complicated subject with a lot of options. If you receive a booklet entitled "Medicare & You" The Official U.S. Government Medicare Handbook, take the time to read the handbook even if you just scan it. If you do not receive a booklet before you turn 65, request a copy from Medicare.gov or call (800) 633-4227.

In this chapter, the following topics concerning health care in retirement will be discussed:
- Healthcare in America
- Medicare parts and plans
- Medicaid nursing home coverage

Nobody expects you to become a Medicare expert, but knowledge is power. You need to know what Medicare does and does not cover to save you from highly elevated blood pressure later on.

1. HEALTHCARE IN AMERICA

America is again Number One, only this time when it comes to spending per person on health care compared to other industrialized countries. Not a great honor.

Canadians spend 60 percent per resident on health care compared to the United States. Germans spend 56 percent of what Americans spend on healthcare and residents in the United Kingdom spend only 42 percent of what we do. Americans are ranked Number 26 in average mortality, so we pay twice as much as residents of other countries to be substantially less healthy than most other developed nations. When it comes to healthcare in America, you do not get what you paid for.

COVID-19 has reduced our life expectancy in America. According to the Centers for Disease Control and Prevention (CDC) Vital Statistics Rapid Release Report No. 010 issued in February 2021, "In the first half of 2020, life expectancy at birth for the total U.S.

population was 77.8 years, declining by 1.0 year from 78.8 years in 2019."

The above CDC Report No. 010 also stated: "Life expectancy for males was 75.1 years in the first half of 2020, representing a decline of 1.2 years from 76.3 years in 2019. For females, life expectancy declined to 80.5 years, decreasing 0.9 year from 81.4 years in 2019."

If you plan to live long enough to enjoy some (or all) of your wealth, then you need to plan to spend some of your wealth on health care. This is especially true while you are in retirement since logically, as you get older, more body parts stop working and replacement parts, if available, are prohibitively expensive and usually come with transplant risks.

How much might you need for health care? One company recently estimated that the average American will spend approximately $200,000 for their health care after age 65. Not only do you need to save to have those funds in retirement, but you also need to employ them effectively to be able to afford comprehensive health care throughout your life.

2.   MEDICARE PARTS AND PLANS

Medicare is the health care plan run by the U.S. Government though the U.S. Department of Health and Human Services. Much of the information in this Section comes from "Medicare & You" which is published by the U.S. Department of Health and Human Services. You have paid for that very informative booklet with your tax dollars. As previously mentioned, if you are sent a copy, read it. Request a copy if you have not received it or somehow misplaced it.

Medicare is complicated and you need to understand what services are covered so you can dispute denials of payment if and when they come.

Medicare coverage is not limited to elderly individuals since it provides health care to people who are disabled and are receiving Social Security.

Medicare has multiple programs which cover different costs. In very general terms, Medicare Part A covers hospitalization, Part B covers doctor visits, Part C is an HMO with more coverage, but fewer choices of providers and Part D covers drugs. Details about the coverage each Medicare Part provides are listed later in this chapter.

Enrollment Deadlines

Some people automatically are enrolled in Medicare including individuals who are disabled and receiving Social Security, people receiving Railroad Retirement Board (RRB) benefits and people who have ALS (also known as Lou Gehrig's disease).

The Initial Enrollment Period for Medicare starts three months before the month you turn 65 and ends three months after the month you turn 65. Even though you have seven months to enroll in Medicare, selecting option coverage can be complicated so avoid waiting until the end of the period.

Contact www.ssa.gov/medicareonly/ or call (800) 772-1213 to obtain more information about Medicare.

If you fail to sign up for Medicare Part A and/or Part B during the Initial Enrollment Period, there is a General Enrollment Period between January 1 and March 31 each year. However, your health care coverage will not start until July 1 of that year. You might also have to pay a higher premium for Part A and/or Part B if you delay enrolling.

Once you are enrolled in Medicare, you can change your coverage during the Annual Election Period which runs between October 15 and December 7. Changes usually involve joining Medicare Advantage or changing your Part D prescription drug coverage,

Medicare currently has four parts: A, B, C and D. Congress will undoubtedly modify Medicare since the Medicare program is projected to run out of money within 10 years if not changed and after Medicare Parts A to D, they still have 22 letters left to play with.

Medicare Part A. – Hospitalization

According to the Department of Health & Human Services, Medicare Part A coverage includes:

- Inpatient care in a hospital
- Inpatient care in a skilled nursing facility (not custodial or long-term care)
- Hospice care
- Home health care
- Inpatient care in a religious nonmedical health care institution

Medicare Part A does NOT cover custodial care at a nursing home. Neither do Medicare parts B, C and D. Custodial care is long-term care for individuals who require assistance with

Medicare Part B – Doctor Visits

Medicare Part B, according to DHHS, coverage includes:
- Medically necessary doctors' services
- Outpatient care
- Home health services
- Durable medical equipment
- Mental health services

Medicare Part B primarily covers doctor visits, and you have to pay for Part B separately. Unlike Part A where you are automatically enrolled once you turn 65, you SHOULD sign up for Part B.

Medicare Part C – Advantage / HMO

Medicare Part C is called Medicare Advantage. Coverage is provided by private insurance companies that are approved by Medicare.

Coverage under Medicare Advantage (Part C) includes:
- All services covered under Medicare Part A
- Part B
- Part D prescription drug coverage
- Possible additional coverage for vision care, dental, hearing and other programs

In exchange for having access to a wider range of services, Medicare Advantage programs have restrictions on the care you can receive.

As explained by DDHS: "If you go to a doctor, other health care provider, facility, or supplier that doesn't belong to the plan's network for non-emergency or non-urgent care services, your services might not be covered, or your costs could be higher. In most cases, this applies to Medicare Advantage HMOs and PPOs."

Medicare Part D – Drugs

As people get older and their health declines, their doctors frequently prescribe more drugs. In theory, Medicare Part D enables a patient on Medicare to save money since covered drugs are available. The reason for the qualifier "in theory" is because for many drugs, there are copayments and deductibles.

Unlike Medicare Part B, which is based on earned income, the premium for Medicare Part D depends on multiple factors including which drugs you are taking. Since the drugs you are taking could change, it is important to review your Part D coverage annually to make sure you have the most cost-effective plan.

3. MEDICAID NURSING HOME COVERAGE

Most Americans will qualify for Medicare once they reach age 65. But Medicare does not pay for custodial nursing home care which is what most people need when they develop illnesses like dementia or suffer strokes requiring on-going nursing care.

The joint federal and state program that might pay for custodial nursing home care is Medicaid which is supposedly reserved for lower income individuals. In order to qualify for Medicaid, you need to have less than $2,000 of countable resources. States decide many of the rules concerning Medicaid so the definition of what is a countable resource varies.

As part of the Patient Protection and Affordable Care Act (also known as Obamacare), Medicaid eligibility was expanded to include people whose annual income is below 138 percent (138%) of the federal poverty level which is $26,347 for a family of three and $15,417 for a single person. Not all states have expanded Medicaid due to concerns about the cost of providing care.

Currently there are lawsuits pending regarding the expansion of Medicaid and Obamacare. Court decisions will inevitably impact coverage so make sure you are making decisions based on current regulations.

Although Medicaid is intended for individuals with low incomes and few resources, some people will try to qualify for nursing home coverage under Medicaid by structuring their assets to become eligible, this is a complicated administrative and ethical matter that is beyond the scope of this book. If you have questions of Medicaid eligibility and prefer not to address those issues with the people who administer Medicaid, then consider contacting an experienced elder law attorney who is knowledgeable of the current regulations in your state.

CHAPTER SUMMARY

Americans pay the most per person for health care in the world, but we are not even in the Top 25 countries for average mortality. Medicare includes Part A (hospitalization); Part B (doctor visits); Part C (Advantage HMO or PPO); and Part D (prescription drugs). Medicaid is a health care program intended to provide medical care to low-income individuals. It is possible to have long-term nursing home care paid for by Medicaid but to be eligible, your income must be low, and you can only have a limited amount of countable assets.

TAKE ACTION

- Sign up for Medicare during your seven-month Initial Enrollment Period that starts three months before your 65th birthday and ends three months after the month you turned 65.
- Carefully review the coverage under Medicare Parts A, B, C and D before you enroll. While you can later change to a different plan and coverage, you have the most options open to you during your Initial Enrollment Period.
- Before planning to rely on Medicaid as your future provider of long-term custodial care, consider discussing what it takes to qualify for Medicaid with an attorney familiar with elder care.

Chapter 18 – Income Distributions

"The problem today is not a lack of proper resources,
but a lack of proper distribution."
Mahatma Gandhi

CHAPTER PREVIEW

Income distributions are a third category you need to manage in
retirement as you strive to better EMPLOY your wealth.

In Chapter 3, we discussed the multiple opportunities to save for
your retirement. Most contributions to a retirement plan are made on
a pre-tax basis. That means you get a tax break up front since the
amount you contribute to your retirement plan is deducted from the
income you pay tax on.

However, no free lunches are served at the IRS Café. While you
are given a tax break when you contribute to a retirement plan, income
taxes are due when the funds are taken out of the plan. The income
and gains are "tax-deferred" rather than tax-free.

One of the major reasons 401(k) and 403(b) plans, along with
traditional IRAs are attractive is that you can invest when you are
working so that you can withdraw funds in retirement when you
expect to be in a lower tax bracket. How and when you withdraw
retirement funds from your accounts can have a huge impact on your
ability to GET wealth.

In this chapter, three aspects of retirement income distributions
will be discussed:
- Expenses when retired
- Retirement account withdrawals
- Retirement income taxation

1. EXPENSES WHEN RETIRED

How much monthly income will you need once you retire? Estimates are all over the map because everyone views their needs differently. You might be planning to travel extensively once you are retired. Other people plan to sell their large home, downsize to a smaller condo in a warmer location and instead of traveling, just enjoy their new home base. While lifestyles differ, major expenses in retirement will usually include health care, housing and living expenses.

Healthcare Expenses

Many people assume that once they turn 65 and qualify for Medicare, all their healthcare expenses will now be completely covered. As we discussed in Chapter 17, Medicare covers some but not nearly all of the healthcare costs for seniors.

Once you turn 65, you get to play Medicare Wheel of Fortune. Tell Vanna you want an A, B, C or D for each one of the Medicare parts. Even if Part A (hospitalization) is being paid for out of tax revenue, you still have to pay for medical expenses not covered by Medicare. It has been estimated that an average married couple age 65 will spend nearly $300,000 on healthcare while retired. Medicare is not a free ticket to the Take-All-You-Want HealthCare Buffet.

Housing Expenses

Another major expense is housing. Recent studies indicate that a large number of retirees still have an outstanding mortgage. Why? When your income is lower in retirement, you should have eliminated as much debt as possible.

According to the Harvard Joint Center for Housing studies, only 25% of homeowners in their late 60's to late 70's still had a mortgage 30 years ago but in 2019, 50% did. Just 3% of people who turned 80 used to have outstanding mortgages while today it is one of every four seniors.

You obviously need to live somewhere in retirement and not having to make a mortgage payment can give you peace of mind.

Granted there are multiple expenses to maintain a house but there are more tax advantages associated with owning rather than renting. With mortgage interest rates at historically low levels, a majority of homeowners should be focused on having a paid-off mortgage once they are retired. Long before you retire, you can plan what your housing costs will be. You cannot know your future health care needs and expenses.

Living Expenses

There is a difference between living and surviving. When you are retired and no longer working, how will you spend your free time? There is a bumper sticker which says: "I am spending my children's inheritance."

Entertainment is rarely free even when you are at home. At one time, television was free other than the cost of electricity and aluminum foil for rabbit ear antennas. In retirement, you may feel the absolute need to pay monthly for cable, streaming programming from Netflix, Disney + and Amazon plus internet service that many third world governments cannot obtain.

2. RETIREMENT ACCOUNT WITHDRAWALS

Retirement accounts are supposed to be long-term investments. Congress has provided great opportunities to save by allowing plan participants to deduct most contributions to 401(k), 403(b) or some other retirement plans. Not only do you reduce your taxable income, but the money you invest in your retirement accounts can grow tax-deferred until taken out. You receive a tax-deduction for your contribution unless you are contributing to the Roth option in your retirement plan account administered by your employer's plan administrators.

But with every tax break comes rules and penalties for breaking those rules. In the case of retirement plans and accounts, withdrawing your funds early prior to 59½ can result in substantial penalties. On the other end of the field, if you do not take out the required minimum amount mandated by the IRS after you have turned 72, again there are substantial penalties. Know and follow the rules.

Early Withdrawal Penalties

Retirement plans like 401(k)s and retirement accounts like IRAs offer tremendous opportunities to save. But in exchange for the up-front tax deductions and the tax-deferred compounding, severe penalties are imposed if you withdraw funds from these accounts before you turn 59½. Penalties are also triggered by early withdrawals from tax-deferred annuities and life insurance products as well.

The penalty for early withdrawals is ten percent (10%) of the amount withdrawn plus ordinary income taxes. Congress passed the CARES Act to temporarily suspend RMDs in 2020 for people.

EXAMPLE 1: Bill is a 55-year-old married individual who recently started his own company. Bill and his wife Mary are in the 22% tax bracket. He needs working capital to purchase equipment and is unable to obtain a business loan since the company has no credit record. Bill decides to withdraw $10,000 from his IRA and feels he will be able to save more in the future when his new company is in the S & P 500. Because Bill is not yet 59½ when he takes the $10,000 out of his IRA, he will pay the IRS an early withdrawal penalty of $1,000 (10% of $10,000) plus income taxes on the $10,000.

Cares Act of 2020

In early 2020, the Coronavirus Aid, Relief and Economic Security (CARES) Act became law. To help individuals suffering economic hardship due to COVID 19, the CARES Act made several changes to the rules involving withdrawals from retirement plans.

Individuals who are not yet 59½, are diagnosed with COVID 19, have a spouse or child with COVID-19 or have been otherwise impacted by the virus can withdraw up to $100,000 from qualified retirement accounts by individuals without incurring the previous 10% penalty.

Section 72(t) transfers

If you do not qualify under the CARES Act to withdraw funds penalty-free from your retirement plan, one way to avoid the 10% early withdrawal penalty is to take advantage of Section 72(t) transfers. Individuals who are not yet 59½ can receive regularly scheduled payments based on the IRA owner's life expectancy and pay income taxes but not the 10% early withdrawal penalty. Once activated, payments must continue for at least five years or until the IRA owner turns 59½, which event occurs last. Withdrawals using 72(t) can only be made from IRAs and not from employer-sponsored 401(k) or 403(b) plans.

EXAMPLE 2: Mary is a recent widow who is 56 years old. She has rolled her deceased spouse's 401(k) into an IRA. Since Mary is not yet 59½, taking funds from her IRA would result in a 10% early withdrawal tax penalty. Mary elects a 72(t) transfer which permits her to receive monthly payments from her IRA based on her life expectancy. Mary is required to continue to receive the payments for at least five years at which time she can take lump sums from her IRA without incurring the 10% tax penalty because she is over 59½.

Required Minimum Distributions (RMDs)

Prior to the passage of the SECURE Act of 2019, individuals had to withdraw a minimum amount based on their age starting when they turn 70½. The SECURE Act delayed until age 72 when certain individuals have to take their required minimum distributions. Individuals who turned 70½ on or before 12/31/2019, have to follow the old rule and take withdrawals at 70½.

The CARES Act of 2020 eliminated the need to take RMDs in 2020 in light of COVID-19. Individuals who were over 70½ on or before 12/31/2019 have to resume taking their RMDs in 2021. People who turn 70½ after 12/31/2019 do not have to start taking RMDs until the year they turn 72.

The penalty for not taking an RMD is very substantial. If you do not take your RMD by the deadline, a fifty percent (50%) excess accumulation penalty is imposed on the amount not taken. The IRS wants you to withdraw money from your tax-deferred retirement plans and accounts and a 50% penalty effectively catches the attention of most taxpayers.

You calculate your RMD on the value of each of your tax-deferred accounts as of 12/31 of the prior year. There are some exceptions for retirement accounts if you are still working past age 71. Check with the plan administrator for your employer's retirement plan. You do not have to take an RMD from each account as long as the total amount you withdraw is greater than or equal to the total of the RMDs for all your impacted accounts.

3. RETIREMENT INCOME TAXATION

It is important to understand what taxes are imposed on the main sources of income in retirement: Social Security, retirement accounts and investments.

Social Security Taxation

A person might retire at 62 and needs income immediately. They could start drawing on Social Security, but the amount could be the lowest figure they would receive. Although there might be adjustments for inflation, given the prospect of being retired for 25 or more years, is there a better choice?

One option would be to postpone taking Social Security until Full Retirement Age or even at age 70 if you can wait that long. As previously indicated in Chapter 16, your monthly Social Security payment increases by 8 percent per year between 66 and 70. So you could receive 132% of your Full Retirement amount if you postpone activating your social security payment until you turn 70.

Paying bills before age 70

Remember the discussion in Chapter 3 about the need for retirement funds? If you have funds in an IRA for example, you can withdraw those funds after age 59½ without the 10% tax penalty. At age 72 you are required to start taking withdrawals from your IRAs so why not start early and decide how much to take out based on your needs and the tax consequences.

At age 72, required IRA distributions are based on your life expectancy. The older you get, the shorter your life expectancy (number of years you are likely to live). As you age, the amount you are required to take out will increase. Unless the remaining funds in your IRA increase due to positive markets that cover the required withdrawals, the value of your IRA will decrease over your lifetime.

Fortunately, the very strong stock market returns since 2008 have in some years more than replaced the value of withdrawals. Do not count on this happening forever.

Determine what your monthly payment would be from Social Security at your Full Retirement Age. Between your Full Retirement Age and when you turn 70, your Social Security increases at 8% percent per year. To get the higher payment (132%) at age 70, consider taking funds out of your IRA equal to what you would have received in Social Security had you activated at Full Retirement Age.

Once you turn 70, start taking the higher payments from Social Security and reduce the amount you are taking from your IRA by the amount you are now receiving annually from Social Security. Not only will you (or your surviving spouse in certain cases) receive the maximum payment permitted, but by reducing withdrawals from your IRA, you allow your IRA to possibly grow to provide additional income for future higher expenses.

Retirement plan taxation

Distributions from tax-deferred retirement plans, retirement accounts and annuities are taxed as ordinary income. Because withdrawals from tax-deferred investments and accounts are taxed at the same rates as your earned income, you should try and delay taking distributions from retirement sources until you are retired and in a lower tax bracket.

EXAMPLE 2: John is 65 years old and still working and is in the 22% tax bracket. Because he is over 59½ he is able to withdraw money from his IRA without incurring a 10% early withdrawal penalty. Rather than take out a car loan which he could afford, John withdraws money from his IRA and pays 22% in taxes to the IRS. Had he waited until his retirement when his tax bracket dropped to 12%, he would have sent substantially less of the IRA withdrawal to the IRS.

Where you live has an impact on the possible state taxation of your retirement benefits. If a substantial amount of your income in retirement will be from sources that are subject to taxation, consider moving to a more tax-friendly state if you were already thinking about relocating.

An article posted on www.aarp.org on 7/30/2020 identified 12 states which do not tax retirement plan distributions: "Nine of those states that don't tax retirement plan income simply have no state income taxes at all: Alaska, Florida, Nevada, New Hampshire, South Dakota, Tennessee, Texas, Washington and Wyoming. The remaining three – Illinois, Mississippi and Pennsylvania – don't tax distributions from 401(k) plans, IRAs or pensions. Alabama and Hawaii don't tax pensions but do tax distributions from 401(k) plans and IRAs."

Investment taxation

Back in Chapter 2, we discussed tax-favored investments like qualified dividends and capital gains. Once you are retired, investment income can be an important source to provide financial security.

EXAMPLE 3: George and his wife Mary are retired and together have income which places them in the 12% tax bracket (couples with taxable income in 2021 between $19,901 and $81,050). They earn $3,000 of qualified dividends from ETFs in their after-tax investment account. Because they are in one of the two lowest tax brackets (10% or 12%), they pay zero federal income taxes on the $3,000 of qualified dividends instead of sending $360 (12% of $3,000) to our friends at the IRS.

EXAMPLE 4: Fred is a widower who receives enough income from his pension, Social Security and investments to place him in the 22% tax bracket (single with taxable income between $40,526 and $86,375 in 2021). He sells a parcel of vacant land he bought 10 years ago for a profit of $10,000 which is treated as a capital gain. Although he is in the 22% tax bracket, the $10,000 profit he made will be taxed at 15% instead of 22% since it was a capital gain.

CHAPTER SUMMARY

Expenses in retirement will not automatically go down once you retire. Health care costs are likely to be a much greater concern and will require paying for insurance to avoid massive out of pockets costs. Retirement account withdrawals need to carefully be planned to avoid unnecessary high taxation. Some withdrawals from retirement accounts are required with substantial tax penalties being imposed if rules are not followed. Retirement income taxation can take a large bite out of your retirement savings and Social Security, so planning is critical.

TAKE ACTION

- As you get closer to retirement, pay off as much debt as you can while you are working. Having a paid-off house enables you to better handle unforeseen expenses in retirement like higher health care costs.
- Coordinate when you will start taking Social Security with withdrawals from retirement accounts. Delay taking Social Security as long as possible and instead take withdrawals from retirement accounts to cover expenses until you activate Social Security payments.
- Build an investment account outside of retirement funds to enable you to take advantage of the preferred tax rate available from qualified dividends and capital gains.

Part III: How to **Transfer** Wealth

*"It's not how much money you make, but how much money you
keep, how hard it works for you, and how many generations
you keep it for."*
Robert Kiyosaki

PREVIEW OF PART III – TRANSFER

Transfer is defined by the Merriam-Webster dictionary as: "To
cause to pass from one to another." Once you have attained financial
independence, transferring your wealth to family, charities or friends
gives your beneficiaries the opportunity to also achieve financial
security. Transfers to your favorite non-profit groups enhances your
charitable legacy.

Part Three of this book discusses how to TRANSFER your wealth
by forming a plan, executing estate planning documents to implement
your plan and by leaving a meaningful legacy for your family and
charities.

SECTION CHAPTERS
Section One – Design Your Plan
    Chapter 19 – Why Bother Planning?
    Chapter 20 – Avoiding Probate
    Chapter 21 – Inventory Your Assets
Section Two – Documents You Need
    Chapter 22 – Powers of Attorney
    Chapter 23 – Wills
    Chapter 24 – Trusts
Section Three – Create Your Legacy
    Chapter 25 – Heir Pains
    Chapter 26 – Selecting Charities
    Chapter 27 – Charitable Ways to Give

ESTATE PLANNING POSITIVES

Estate planning is frequently viewed as something to postpone as long as possible since who wants to think about dying other than funeral home directors? But an effective estate plan could provide you with personal protection while you are living in addition to transferring your assets according to your stated wishes after you have died.

If you have worked hard to save, invest and manage your wealth, who is better qualified than you to decide who should receive your assets after your death? Estate planning gives you the great opportunity to not only provide security for your family but also, if you have adequate funds, to fund charities which support those causes that you are passionate about. Your legacy is what you leave behind. How do you hope to be remembered after you die?

Section One: Design Your Estate Plan

Chapter 19 – Why Bother Planning?

"Whatever you want to do, do it now.
There are only so many tomorrows."
Michael Landon

DESIGN YOUR PLAN

Section One on how to TRANSFER your wealth describes how to DESIGN YOUR ESTATE PLAN by addressing the following: 1) Why bother planning? 2) Avoiding probate; and 3) Inventory your assets.

CHAPTER PREVIEW

Do you care about what happens to your assets if you become incapacitated and also after your death? An effective estate plan can give you personal protection during your lifetime and benefits your family after you die. Maybe you trust the probate courts to select the right people to handle your funds if you are disabled and need someone to make medical decisions for you. Maybe you believe that other people make better decisions than you do about your life and your family. Breaking News: While less than 60% of Americans have an estate plan, a shocking 100% of humans will pass away someday.

COVID 19 has clearly shown that life-threatening illnesses can occur regardless of how advanced our healthcare system claims to be. Add natural disasters we cannot control like hurricanes, wildfires and flooding and it should impress upon you that you need to have a plan to transfer your wealth, hopefully many years in the future.

It is estimated that people will spend over 80,000 hours working to earn a living. Allocate a few hours to make sure that the wealth you have worked so hard to earn provides for you during your lifetime and transfers according to your instructions after your death.

In this chapter, three reasons to have an estate plan are discussed:
- Provide lifetime personal protection
- Reduce family disruptions
- Avoid death by probate

1. PROVIDE LIFETIME PERSONAL PROTECTION

Estate planning is not only about transferring assets after you die. The documents we will be discussing in upcoming Chapter 22 (Powers of Attorney - POAs) and Chapter 24 (Trusts) are intended to provide you with personal protection during your lifetime.

Wills (Chapter 23) are dead instruments which only activate when you die. What happens if you are in a car accident and are disabled for three months? You have not died so the person you named as executor or personal representative in your will has no authority to pay your bills or handle other financial matters for you while you are disabled.

General durable powers of attorney (Chapter 22) enable you, not the local probate court, to decide who should handle your financial affairs if you become incapacitated due to stroke, car accident, Alzheimer disease, etc. Powers of attorney (POAs) are the opposite of wills since POAs are only valid while you are alive. When you die, so does your power of attorney.

Revocable "living" trusts (Chapter 24) also can safeguard your assets by making sure your funds are used for your care during your lifetime.

EXAMPLE 1: Boris is having serious health issues and decides he needs to make arrangements to transfer assets to his wife and children after he dies. Boris has his attorney prepare durable powers of attorney authorizing his wife to make financial and medical decisions on his behalf if he is mentally or physically disabled. His attorney also prepares Boris a self-trusteed revocable living trust to make sure assets in his trust are used to care for Boris during his lifetime and transfer to his beneficiaries after he dies.

Design your estate plan to first provide personal protection for you during your lifetime, second to support your family and finally, to transfer your assets after you have died.

2. REDUCE FAMILY DISRUPTION

"Always go to other people's funerals, otherwise they won't come to yours."
Yogi Berra

Family Feud might be entertaining on TV, but family feuds caused by no or poor estate planning are never fun to watch. Even if everyone in your family gets along well now, money can corrupt people worse than power. Without an effective estate plan, other people decide who receives your assets. Nobody should want the loudest person in your family or the individual able to afford the most aggressive lawyers to make decisions regarding your care and who ultimately receives your wealth.

An amazing number of families are torn apart over disputes about estates. Why risk having arguments over who gets grandma's turkey platter which would never get a single bid on eBay and would be rejected as a donation to every charity thrift store. It is not the value of the item being fought over. Possession of certain items are viewed as proving who the deceased loved most.

One of your kids might feel slighted because they were not your first choice to be your personal representative or trustee. But it is far better to have someone experience hurt feelings than to leave matters unresolved so that your hyper-controlling son-in-law does not wind up running the distribution of your estate through your daughter.

EXAMPLE 2: Mary is a widow with four grown children. Mary decides she does not need estate planning documents since all of her children get along well with each other. Mary puts all of her bank accounts in joint name with Sarah, her oldest daughter. Mary tells her children that after Mary dies, Sarah will divide the accounts equally between the four children. Unfortunately, greed is a powerful emotion. After Mary dies, Sarah announces that all of Mary's accounts are joint with rights of survivorship with her and since Sarah is the surviving owner, the funds belong solely to Sarah. Hire the lawyers and start the meters.

While estate planning documents do not eliminate the possibilities of family fights, at least they provide a framework which will hopefully lead to an acceptable outcome.

3. AVOID DEATH BY PROBATE

"I am not afraid of death;
I just don't want to be there when it happens."
Woody Allen

Much has been written about why you should avoid probate. For many people, probate is like the great white shark in the movie Jaws that you sense is approaching but you never see until it rises up to bite you.

Probate is basically the legal transfer of assets. While probate proceedings can resemble the courtroom drama in movies, TV shows and John Grisham novels, probate can also be handled administratively without a trial. Supervised probate involves a judge, lawyers and meds to reduce your blood pressure. Simplified or independent probate is usually much quicker, cheaper and far less contentious and is handled at a counter at the courthouse rather than in front of a judge.

Regardless of the type of probate that may affect your estate, in Chapter 20 we will discuss ways to avoid probate. Again, this will involve implementing a plan of action. But first you have to have a plan.

Not having an estate plan means that laws enacted by your friendly neighborhood state legislature will govern who should receive your wealth. This is not the first choice of most political observers. The more complicated your family situation, the greater the need for estate planning.

EXAMPLE 3: Fred is a single individual, divorced with three adult children by two different spouses. Fred likes to control his life, his finances and his family, which might be why he has been divorced three times. Fred does not trust lawyers (big shock), so he does not have an estate plan. When Fred dies none of his bank or investment accounts are jointly held so a probate court proceeding has been started. Fred's ex-spouses, his children and his grandchildren all claim that Kind Old Fred promised each of them the bulk of his estate. After many billable hours by the lawyers, hopefully there will be enough left over to pay for lunch for the parties that prevail.

To be fair, there are times when probate is beneficial. If someone is manipulated into signing a will or trust which gives assets to the person doing the manipulating, you would be glad to have the option of going to probate court to prove that the will or trust was invalid.

Unfortunately, the more frequent occurrence involves people believing they are entitled to more of an estate than they were given in the estate planning documents. There is an old saying: "Pigs are always hungry."

Probate is like a fire extinguisher. Good to have available if you need it. Even better is to implement a plan that prevents a fire from occurring.

CHAPTER SUMMARY

An estate plan can help you control your assets during your lifetime if you become disabled. With appropriate documents including powers of attorney and trusts, you can provide personal protection for yourself and reduce the likelihood of family conflicts over inheritances. Effective estate planning can also eliminate probate which is both public and usually very expensive in the case of supervised probate.

TAKE ACTION

- Commit to prepare an estate plan for yourself and your spouse if you are married. Ask family and friends if they can recommend an estate planning attorney or research how to prepare documents yourself if cost is an issue.
- Discuss with your family what you intend to do with your assets after you die. Find out while you are living what drama you will miss after you have died.
- Avoid having your family go through probate by having your assets be held jointly where appropriate. Consider placing your assets in a self-trusteed revocable trust if you are single or if you are married and prefer not to have all of your assets held jointly with your spouse or someone else.

Chapter 20 – Avoiding Probate

"Everybody wants to go to heaven,
but nobody wants to die."
Unknown

CHAPTER PREVIEW

Avoiding probate is a second goal you should strive for when designing your estate plan to TRANSFER your wealth.

Individuals sometimes appear to fear probate more than death. By far the most frequently stated goal for estate planning clients is a desire to avoid probate even though most people are not sure what probate is.

For many, probate is like a root canal. You might not be sure what is involved but you know for sure you do not want to experience it.

Probate is the legal process to transfer assets at the time of your death. Based on the negative experiences of many people, probate seems to be the process to transfer assets to attorneys who are more than willing to fight for your right to inherit more money until the money runs out.

There are two types of probate: 1) Supervised probate (what you should try to avoid) and 2) Simplified (or independent) probate. Supervised probate is usually conducted in front of a judge and is expensive and frequently contentious. Simplified probate is usually handled at the counter of the courthouse and is much quicker, cheaper and hopefully keeps your blood pressure under 300 over 120.

Try to stick with simplified probate as the option to be used if needed. Some wills take the opposite view and stipulate that supervised probate is required. Why would you want to start with the more complex and expensive approach? Begin with simplified probate and if circumstances like a will contest develop, then move the process up to more complicated supervised probate.

Once you have simplified probate as the default option in your will, you should then focus your efforts on trying to avoid probate.

In this chapter, three types of ownership that avoid probate will be discussed:

- Jointly held assets
- Beneficiary designations
- Trust held assets

1. JOINTLY HELD ASSETS

One of the most common ways to avoid probate is to hold assets jointly with one person or multiple people. While jointly held assets avoid probate, they have the potential of creating serious ownership problems. There are different forms of joint ownership: 1) Joint tenants with right of survivorship; 2) Tenants by the entirety; and 3) Tenants in common.

Joint tenants with right of survivorship

Joint tenants with right of survivorship is the most common form of joint ownership. The letters JTWROS will sometimes appear on these types of accounts. All the parties on a JTWROS account are equal owners of the assets. When one joint owner dies, the asset transfers to the surviving owner(s) without probate.

EXAMPLE 1: Judy is a widow who has three grown children. Judy handles her own finances like paying her bills but realizes that her health is gradually declining, so she adds her oldest daughter, Cindy as a joint owner on her checking account. If Judy becomes unable to handle her own financial affairs, as a joint owner of the account, Cindy can withdraw funds for her mother's expenses. When Judy dies, the remaining funds in the account transfer to Cindy without going through probate. If Judy wanted the bank account to be divided equally between her three children after her death, she is relying on Cindy to distribute one third of the funds to each of her other two children. Technically, however, Cindy is the surviving owner of the joint account and is entitled to all of the funds.

Besides having funds transfer only to the surviving joint owners of an account, another potential problem with using joint accounts to transfer assets is that all owners named on a joint account have access to the funds. This may be acceptable but there have been circumstances where a joint owner withdraws funds for their personal use contrary to the intent of the other joint owners.

Another problem is that the assets in a joint account could become embroiled in lawsuits involving any of the joint owners. If one owner is going through a divorce, they are required to disclose all assets they hold in joint name. The same asset disclosure requirement would be true for parties who have been sued.

Tenants by the entirety

Tenants by the entirety are similar to joint tenants with right of survivorship except that tenancy by the entirety exists only between spouses. Like joint tenants with right of survivorship between any two people, the surviving spouse inherits the assets without probate. Besides avoiding probate, in some states, tenants by the entirety also receive extremely strong creditor protection. If permitted in your state, assets held by tenants by the entirety might be subject only to claims filed against both spouses. If only one spouse is sued and has a judgement against them, the property held by tenants by the entirety usually cannot be attached.

Couples will sometimes transfer assets into joint trusts. In many states, joint trusts do not offer the same high degree of creditor protection provided by tenants in the entireties. Since assets in a joint trust flow to the surviving beneficiaries, joint trusts operate similar to tenants by the entirety but without the creditor protection.

Some advisors advocate using joint trusts to avoid probate in the event of the simultaneous death of a married couple, which is statistically rare. Instead of one joint trust, having a self-trusteed, revocable living trust for each spouse and assets held jointly by the spouses will frequently provide a better outcome, Trusts will be discussed in greater detail in Chapter 24.

Tenants in common

Unlike assets held jointly with the right of survivorship which transfer without probate to the surviving owners of the assets, the ownership interests of tenants in common do not automatically transfer to the surviving owners upon death. Instead, each tenant in common decides who receives their share according to their estate planning documents or by intestacy if someone dies without a will. Intestacy is governed by state law and might not transfer your share of assets like real estate to the people you prefer.

EXAMPLE 2: John is a widower who owns a lakefront vacation house that has increased substantially in value since he bought it. John wants his three children to own equal shares of the house when he dies. John also wants his grandchildren to inherit their parents' share unless they decide to sell the share. John places the vacation house in his trust with instructions that upon his death, the house is to be divided in as equal shares as possible between his then living descendants. John specifies that his three children will initially own their shares as tenants in common to permit each of his children to transfer ownership of their respective share to whomever they wish.

2. BENEFICIARY DESIGNATIONS

Certain assets like retirement accounts and life insurance death benefits can be paid to individuals or revocable trusts without going through probate. But this requires that the beneficiary designations for those accounts and policies be current and correct. Since life circumstances change (minor children become adults, couples get divorced, named beneficiaries die, etc.) you should review your beneficiary forms periodically to make sure they properly reflect your current goals for those assets.

Retirement Accounts

For many Americans, retirement accounts have become their largest single asset due to the popularity of defined contribution plans like 401(k)s and 403(b)s. According to the Investment Company

Institute, defined contribution plans held $8.2 trillion as of June 19, 2019, and total retirement plan assets were $29.1 trillion. Defined contribution plan assets transfer according to the account beneficiary form unless a federal law takes priority over the form.

Since 401(k) plans are subject to federal regulation by the Employer Retirement Income Security Act of 1974 (ERISA), a current spouse of the plan participant must be named as the primary beneficiary unless the spouse signs off as a beneficiary and their signature is notarized. This is to prevent an employer administered retirement account from going to someone other than a current spouse without the knowledge of the spouse.

EXAMPLE 3: Mary and Scott are married, and this is the second marriage for each of them. They both have children by their prior marriages. Mary and Scott each participate in the 401(k) plans offered by their employers. Mary and Scott have agreed that each of their 401(k)s will transfer to their children from their previous marriages instead of to each other. In order to comply with ERISA, Mary and Scott have to sign forms designating their children as beneficiaries and their signatures must be notarized.

Individual Retirement Accounts – IRAs

IRAs and home equity are now the largest assets in most people's portfolio. With the decline in employer provided pension plans, IRAs held $12.6 trillion in assets as of April 1, 2021.

Given how much of your wealth could be in IRAs, how much attention have you paid to who will receive what remains in your IRAs after you die?

IRAs avoid probate only if you caption the beneficiary designation correctly.

Life Insurance

Life insurance death benefits can avoid probate, again if the beneficiary designations are properly filled out. Leaving the beneficiary designations open will result in the benefits being paid to your estate. Which might result in an unnecessary trip through probate.

EXAMPLE 4: Valarie is a single individual who owns a term life insurance policy in which she is the insured. Valarie names her daughter, Sarah as the first (primary) beneficiary. Valarie names Sarah's two children as the secondary (contingent) beneficiaries. In the event Sarah were to die before Valarie, then the insurance death benefit would be paid equally to Sarah's children without probate.

3. TRUST HELD ASSETS

Assets held in a revocable trust can transfer to a beneficiary without going through probate. After you have accumulated wealth, hopefully you will use and enjoy it. Once you have moved to the Great Beyond (beyond - what?), unless you are a fan of amateur cage fighting, you should try to reduce to hard feelings that will inevitably occur after you die and relatives, friends and estate sale vultures start zeroing in on your "things."

Will that be you turning over in your grave/urn when your least favorite daughter-in-law who cannot cook instant oatmeal claims Grandma's pewter serving platter because you decided you did not need a will since "everybody knows what items they are getting." Right. The serving bowls probably have a negative value on eBay. But many relatives have not spoken to each other for years because they felt they should have gotten a particular item that became a must-have treasure on the show where some antique dealer claims the artifact passed down from a great, great aunt who tended bar at a saloon frequented by the Sundance Kid is now worth more than the Mona Lisa.

Avoid will alternatives like placing "permanent" yellow post-It notes on items indicating who receives the Picasso, who gets the velvet Elvis and who gets Dogs Playing Poker. Permanent?

Do your family and friends a favor and either give items away during your lifetime to those you want to receive them or at least write down your instructions, sign and date the document and give multiple copies to your beneficiaries.

The word "probate" invokes images of children of the deceased fighting in court over who will get the family pewter serving platter and the piles of money Mom promised (everyone?) would go to whomever became the custodian of the pewter serving platter. Emotions are always high when you combine the death of a family member with money.

Some (not all) attorneys who dismiss the goal of bypassing probate frequently are hopeful that the family of the deceased will seek them out to handle the supposedly complex disposition of Aunt Wanda's 50-year-old furniture, matching plastic dust covers, mismatched silverware from opening bank accounts and dishes best used under plastic houseplants.

You need to start planning how to transfer that wealth to someone or some entity. You would be amazed at the number of IRAs without beneficiary designations or IRAs naming a former spouse as a beneficiary.

CHAPTER SUMMARY

Holding assets in joint names with rights of survivorship is one of the most common ways to avoid probate. You can also avoid having your assets transfer via probate by making sure beneficiary designation forms for your life insurance and retirement accounts are not only filled out but reflect your current goals. Trust held assets can also avoid probate and provide you with lifetime control over your funds if you become disabled.

TAKE ACTION

- Confirm with your credit union or bank that all of your accounts are jointly held, have TOD (Transfer on Death) instructions or are held by your self-trusteed, revocable living trust.
- Check that your retirement accounts and your insurance policies all have properly completed beneficiary designation forms on file.

Request written confirmation of who the beneficiaries are and store that information with your estate planning documents.

- If and when you have a self-trusteed, revocable living trust, transfer those assets into the trust that might otherwise be in the sole name of the owner and therefore likely go through probate.

Chapter 21 – Inventory Your Assets

*"Know what you own and know
why you own it."*
Peter Lynch

CHAPTER PREVIEW

Having an inventory of your assets is a critical third goal when you are designing your estate plan to TRANSFER your wealth.

If you were disabled in a car accident, does your family know which credit unions, banks or investment companies you deal with so that they have funds for your care? When you die, does your family know where to go to collect your hard-earned retirement benefits, where to file claims for life insurance benefits and where you keep other assets?

The amount of wealth you have is your business. But knowing the companies that hold your assets is critical information for your spouse, your family or your advisors to know. If you become unable to handle your own financial affairs, how can people access funds for your care if they do not know what companies hold your assets?

In this chapter, we stress the need to have an inventory of the following items:
- Financial assets
- Retirement accounts
- Documents

1. FINANCIAL ASSETS

Financial assets include transaction accounts, investment accounts and life insurance policies. Where are your checking and savings accounts? Do you have brokerage accounts at one or more companies? Who has a list of the companies and account numbers of any life insurance policies you have in place?

Transaction Accounts

Financial accounts include checking and savings accounts. Most individuals have some types of transaction accounts to pay bills. These accounts might be held at banks, credit unions, mutual funds, insurance companies, etc.

The internet has made investing both easier and more complex. Easier because you can painlessly open financial accounts on-line at most financial institutions. More complex because you can have multiple investment accounts without a paper trail. Does anyone know the passwords to your computer so that your financial information can be retrieved when those funds are needed for your care or for your family?

EXAMPLE 1: Fred and Mary are married and have two grown children. Fred and Mary have joint accounts at a local credit union. Fred also has a savings account that he opened online which is in his sole name and for which he receives electronic statements to his computer. He considers it to be his "mad money" so in addition to Mary not being an owner of the account, she is also not aware it exists. Fred dies before Mary and the account is eventually escheated (transferred) to the state because nobody other than Fred knew about it. Eight years after Fred dies, one of his children enters Fred's name on www.unclaimed.org, discovers the account and files a claim to recover it.

If you do have transaction accounts in your sole name, let someone (your spouse, children, CPA or attorney) know which financial institutions hold the funds. Should you want to keep the account a secret, at least include a death beneficiary using a caption like TOD (Transfer on Death or POD (Pay On Death) as previously discussed in Chapter 20 to avoid probate.

Investment Accounts

Investment accounts include items like mutual funds you hold directly with the fund company. You might also have a brokerage account where you buy stocks and exchange traded funds (ETFs).

Since some investors are aggressive stock traders while others buy and hold mutual funds or ETFs for several years, individuals have opted not to have certain investments accounts held jointly.

As more wealth is transferred from elderly parents to their adult children, there is also a trend to keep certain assets in the sole name of the person receiving the inheritance. With the increase in second and sometimes third marriages, individuals might prefer not to have all their assets be in joint accounts and instead hold assets in a self-trusteed, revocable living trust. See Chapter 24 for more information on trusts.

EXAMPLE 2: Julie received a small inheritance when her grandmother died. Following her grandmother's wishes, Julie invested the inheritance in a growth mutual fund and opts to have all dividends reinvested by purchasing more shares of the fund. Julie gives the tax statements she receives from the mutual fund to her tax preparer every year but otherwise just files them away. When Julie nears retirement, she reviews her mutual fund statement and is pleased to learn that her small inheritance has grown substantially. Julie adds the mutual fund to her inventory of assets.

Even if you want to keep an investment account a secret, maintain a record of where you invest. Also, if you prefer to have the account in your sole name, include a beneficiary by adding a transfer on death (TOD) provision to your account. A TOD designation will not help you if you become disabled, but it will avoid probate, assuming someone knows the accounts exists and files a claim. An even better option is to put the account in your self-trusteed revocable trust (Chapter 24).

Life Insurance Policies

Life insurance has become an important employee benefit at many large companies. Frequently, employees receive life insurance with a death benefit equal to a certain percentage of a person's salary. But if you are no longer working at the company where you previously had life insurance and have insurance policies elsewhere, it is much harder for your family and beneficiaries of those policies to know where to file a claim after you die.

Many years ago, it was common to use one person or agency for most of your insurance. Now that life insurance is frequently an employee benefit.

60 Minutes aired a story which found that $7.5 billion (with a B) of life insurance is never collected. Beneficiaries cannot file claims on policies they do not know exist.

EXAMPLE 3: When Jack turned 18, Jack's grandfather paid for Jack to take out a life insurance policy on Jack's life. Given his young age, the premiums on the policy were relatively low so the policy was paid up in a few years and no further premiums were required. Jack's grandfather died several years ago, and Jack forgot about the policy. When Jack dies, nobody knows to file a claim for the death benefits.

In the event you need to find out if there are in force insurance policies for someone else (estate settlement, etc.), consider contacting MIB Group, Inc. It is a collection of 400 plus insurance companies. For a $75 fee, they will scan all applications filed since 1996 to see if there are any policies in the name of the person.

2. RETIREMENT ACCOUNTS

It used to be a lot easier to know where a person's retirement accounts were. People worked at the same large company or institution for 20 plus years and qualified for a pension when they retired. Most companies have ended their traditional pension plans in favor of defined contribution plans which permit former employees to move their retirement assets to several options outside of the company's plan after they retire.

EXAMPLE 3: Sue worked at a small hospital for six years when she first graduated from college. That hospital eventually merged into a large medical system. She accepted a position at a larger hospital system where she worked for 20 years before retiring. Sue regularly had part of her paycheck deposited into her employer's 403(b) plan which she rolled into an IRA after she retired. She was recently contacted by the HR department of her first employer and was pleased to learn that she was entitled to a small pension based on her six years of service. Although not a large amount, she earned it and was fortunate she received notification about the benefit.

Some individuals decide to transfer their retirement plan assets when they leave a company. If you are moving to a new company which does not offer a retirement plan or the plan at your new employer is far worse than the plan at the company you left, then keep it where it is. Make sure you advise the former employer of any address changes so that you are always receiving your statements. Having your statements sent to you electronically would solve this problem.

But make sure you are letting someone know your passwords so that they can access your account if needed. There are services that will keep this information if you do not have someone you would trust with your passwords.

EXAMPLE 4: Bill is a single individual whose technical skills are in high demand. Bill frequently changes jobs and transfers to another part of the country. Although Bill always contributes to the 401(k) or 403(b) plans wherever he works, he never says long enough at any one company for the balances in any one retirement account to be very large and never transfers his old accounts. Bill passes away in a car accident and his family has no records of his multiple retirement accounts. His accounts are escheated to the state where each plan custodian has their headquarters.

Working at the same company for 30 plus years is no longer given merger-activated downsizing, recession driven lay-offs and a desire by younger workers to switch jobs frequently to learn new skills in new locations for higher compensation. Job jumping makes sense if you also transfer your retirement funds when you leave a company.

3. DOCUMENTS

Where do you keep important records like copies of tax returns and deeds to real estate you own?   Do you have a file cabinet where you keep important documents? If it is locked, who has a key? Who has a back-up key? If you do not trust anyone (very sad) then consider keeping keys and combinations at a safe deposit box at a bank or credit union. Make your self-trusteed, revocable living trust the account owner of the safe deposit box.

If you keep your important papers in a safe at your home, where do you keep a copy of the combination? What happens when you are incapacitated or dead? Assuming Madam Zelda the Spiritualist is unable to contact you, the safe will have to be broken into if nobody knows the combination.

EXAMPLE 3: Bob takes pride in the fact that he has never thrown out any of the statements or printed material he has received from the several companies he has investments with. The problem is that over the past 40 years, Bob has accumulated so much paperwork that much of it is just thrown into unmarked boxes in his basement. Bob does not want any one person to know all his business, so nobody does. Other than threatening to report him to the local fire marshal, Bob's wife has given up trying to get Bob organized. When Bob dies, important papers are buried with outdated reports and get thrown out by frustrated family members trying to organize the mess.

The only thing worse than keeping no records is keeping every piece of paper you have ever received regarding your financial accounts. Find a middle ground to sort out what is current and important. Save a few thousand trees by recycling as much paper as you can. Request electronic reports where available.

CHAPTER SUMMARY

Financial assets like bank accounts and life insurance can be moved between institutions. Account balances change but your financial assets usually remain at the same companies. Retirement account statements have gone paperless at many companies, so the previous paper trail no longer exists. Documents like tax returns and property deeds need to be kept in a safe place that your family or advisors know about.

TAKE ACTION

- Create and periodically update a list of all the banks, credit unions and financial institutions where you have transaction accounts. Include a list of the insurance policies you own or have as an employee benefit. Share a copy of the list with someone you trust or whoever you name as the personal representatives of your will and /or successor trustees of your revocable living trust.
- Prepare and share an inventory of your retirement accounts. After you leave an employer, transfer your retirement to the plan administered by your current employer if the investment choices and administrative fees are comparable or to an IRA if the benefits outweigh a transfer to another employer-sponsored plan.
- Keep all your important records and legal documents in one location. Make sure the records and documents are in waterproof containers or otherwise safeguarded. If you prefer storing items in a fireproof safe or locked file cabinet, decide how you are going to provide someone access to the contents if you become disabled and after you die.

Section Two: Documents You Need

Chapter 22 – Powers of Attorney

"Surround yourself with great people; delegate authority;
and get out of the way."
Ronald Reagan

DOCUMENTS YOU NEED

Section Two on how to TRANSFER your wealth describes the following legal DOCUMENTS YOU NEED as part of an effective estate plan: 1) Powers of attorney; 2) Wills; and 3) Trusts.

CHAPTER PREVIEW

Powers of attorney are the first documents you need as part of your estate plan.

People frequently think that estate planning only deals with transferring assets after you die. Effective estate planning also involves making sure you retain control of your assets during your lifetime and includes documents which indicate the type and amount of healthcare you should receive if you cannot make medical decisions for yourself. After your death, estate planning helps to transfer your wealth with hopefully minimal delays, costs and drama.

If you become disabled (car accident, serious illness, operation, etc.) who would you want to handle your financial affairs like banking transactions and the possible sale of real estate you own? A power of attorney (POA) gives someone the "power" to act on behalf of the person who authorized the POA.

In this chapter, three types of powers of attorney will be discussed:
- General durable powers of attorney
- Springing durable powers of attorney
- Health care durable powers of attorney

1. GENERAL DURABLE POWERS OF ATTORNEY

A durable power of attorney can be far more important than having a will. A durable power of attorney (POA) is valid while you are alive and terminates at your death. A will is the opposite of a POA since a will does not activate and become effective until you die. That is why an estate plan should include powers of attorney and a will along with a revocable trust if appropriate.

Do not ignore the possibility of becoming disabled during your lifetime. Over 61 million adults in the United States have some type of disability, according to a 2019 report by the Centers of Disease Control and Prevention (CDC). The report further indicates that: "2 in 5 adults age 65 years and older have a disability." As you become older and health issues are more of a concern, the need increases for a durable power of attorney. A durable POA gives someone the "power" to act on your behalf. A POA is "durable" because it continues to be valid even after a person is incapacitated.

The person who has the POA prepared is the principal. The person given the authority to sign the name of the principal is called an agent or attorney in fact. A power of attorney gives a tremendous amount of authority to another person so executing a POA should not be taken lightly. However, if you do not appoint someone to act for you, then you run the risk of having the local probate court do it. Your choice.

A person who signs a durable POA and subsequently develops dementia or is otherwise incapacitated could have their durable POA used to authorize payment for medical care for that individual. The durable POA could also be used to handle other financial matters like applying for employee benefits and making bank deposits and withdrawals.

The benefit of having a POA is not limited to situations where the principal becomes disabled. Healthy people will sometimes use a

POA to appoint a person to represent them at a real estate closing in another state when they are unable (or chose not) to attend.

EXAMPLE 1: Earl travels extensively overseas in conjunction with his job. While he is out of the country, Earl sometimes is sent documents that require his signature. Earl signs a general durable power of attorney effective upon execution in which he names his wife, Judy as his agent. Judy uses the POA to sign documents on Earl's behalf when he is out of town. Earl also executes a limited power of attorney giving his CPA the authority to represent him at a tax hearing. The POA only allows his CPA to handle the tax matters. Unlike the general power of attorney naming Judy to act, the limited power of attorney is restricted to a specific purpose.

The greatest drawback to POAs is that the agents you select in your durable POA might use the document to benefit themselves. While it is hard to believe that someone you trust would steal from you, money can be a very powerful drug. You need to select agents that you strongly believe will always act in your best interests.

Some states have laws which require that before your agent can act on your behalf, they have to sign a document agreeing to provide the principal with an accounting of their actions. These documents also clearly state that your agent is liable to you for misusing the POA.

Also, there are no guarantees that institutions like banks, credit unions, HR departments, etc. will honor the durable POA and permit the agent to carry out the actions needed by the principal. Before it is needed, it is advisable to present the durable POA to those institutions (bank, real estate title company, etc.) who might be asked to rely on a POA to see if they want additional provisions added in order for them to accept the authority of the agent.

2. SPRINGING DURABLE POWERS OF ATTORNEY

A general durable power of attorney (above) usually is effective upon execution, which means that as soon as the POA is signed, the agent or attorney in fact is able to act.

Some people, however, are reluctant to give anyone general authority over their financial affairs until they are unable to act for themselves. An elderly person might realize their health is failing but feel they are currently still able to make financial decisions for themselves and are reluctant to give up control until they absolutely need help.

A springing durable power of attorney becomes effective when certain conditions are met, not when the POA is signed by the principal. Those conditions might consist of something like two medical physicians, one of whom is the personal doctor of the principal, providing written documentation that the principal is no longer to act for themselves. That triggers the "springing" of the POA.

EXAMPLE 2: Mary is a widow with four children. She does not want to give one of her children the authority to act under a general durable power of attorney that is effective upon execution. Instead, Mary signs a springing power of attorney which provides that the POA activates if two physicians, one of whom is Mary's personal doctor, indicates that she is unable to act for herself.

As previously mentioned, some institutions are reluctant to permit an agent to act under a power attorney. They might insist on receiving proof that the principal is still alive or that the conditions authorizing the springing has actually taken place.

As will be discussed in upcoming Chapter 24, for those reasons, it is frequently advisable to also execute a revocable trust. A trustee is held to a higher fiduciary standard which might convince the financial institution which is otherwise reluctant to act to honor a request made by an acting trustee.

3. DURABLE POWERS OF ATTORNEY FOR HEALTH CARE

A medical power of attorney is sometimes referred to as a living will. A medical POA permits you to decide who is to speak and act for you regarding your health care if you are disabled. This POA is an extremely important document to have as you get older and health issues become more of a concern.

As a larger number of Americans are over the age of 70, dementia has significantly increased. According to the Alzheimer's Association, they estimate that currently, 5.8 million Americans 65 or older have Alzheimer's dementia. By 2050, they estimate that approximately 13.8 million American age 65 or older will have Alzheimer's dementia.

The person who prepares a medical power of attorney is again called a principal. The principal designates an agent (also known as a patient advocate) to make medical decisions for the principal.

Terri Schiavo Case

The problem of not having a medical POA was famously exposed in the Terry Schiavo case in Florida several years ago. Ms. Schiavo suffered cardiac arrest at age 26 in 1990. She suffered massive brain damage and was declared to be in a persistent vegetative state. Her husband asked the courts to withdraw life support while Terri Schiavo's parents felt she was not ready to die. The resulting public circus included multiple state court lawsuits, hearings in the Florida State Legislature, five lawsuits in Federal Court and four rejections by the U.S. Supreme Court to review the case. Ultimately courts authorized the removal of her feeding tube and Terri Schiavo died on 3/31/2005, more than 15 years after the heart attack that left her in a persistent vegetative state.

Regardless of your personal feelings regarding the Terri Schiavo case and others like it, this should have been a private matter decided by the client/patient and not a public battle.

Medical powers of attorney usually include end of life care decisions. If you are in a coma, you should determine how much medical care you would want to receive before your patient advocate authorized the withdrawal of life support.

EXAMPLE 3: Barb is a retired single individual who is experiencing health problems. Barb signs a medical durable power of attorney naming her niece, Deborah as her patient advocate. Six months later,

Barb suffers a stroke and is temporarily incapacitated. Deborah has the authority to make decisions regarding Barb's health care involving the assisted living facility she is moved to along with the physical therapy Barb now requires.

If you prefer not to hire an attorney to prepare a medical durable power of attorney, many public libraries have copies available. Make sure that you follow the instructions regarding who can witness your signature.

CHAPTER SUMMARY

A general durable power of attorney is usually effective upon execution and enables you to appoint someone to act on your behalf if you are unable to handle primarily financial matters for yourself. A springing durable power of attorney is not effective until certain conditions are met such as two doctors providing documents saying you are disabled. Durable powers of attorney for health care, sometimes also referred to as living wills, enable you to designate a patient advocate to make decisions involving your medical care if you are unable to make those decisions for yourself.

TAKE ACTION

- If you have someone who you absolutely trust, name that individual to be your agent in a durable power of attorney. Should you be fortunate enough to have multiple people who you trust, then name then as alternates agents in a durable power of attorney in order of preference.
- In the event that you only want a power of attorney to be activated if and when you become incapacitated, then sign a springing power of attorney.
- Decide who you would want to make medical decisions involving your health care on your behalf if you cannot act. Execute a medical power of attorney designating and at least one alternate if your first choice is unable or unwilling to act.

Chapter 23 – Wills

"Where there is a will, I want to be in it."
Unknown

CHAPTER PREVIEW

A will is the second document you need as part of your estate plan to TRANSFER your wealth.

When most people think about estate planning, the focus is always on a will. While a will is an important part of a comprehensive estate plan, it is just that – a part of an estate plan.

Wills are frequently the star attraction in movies that seem to portray family members as amateur cage fighters, without the cage. Name a movie where the will actually brings a family together?

The Reading of the Will in a dark wood paneled lawyer's office has all the pageantry and unfortunate results as what occurred with the opening of the Ark of the Covenant in the first Indiana Jones movie. For the record, there are male attorneys who are under 80 years old and still have hair. In fact, an increasing number of attorneys and judges are women. After watching the verbal food fights that result from a Reading of the Will, does anyone wonder why over 60% of Americans die without a will?

Despite their terrible reputation as a peacemaker, wills help people transfer assets from an owner to beneficiaries when the owner of the assets dies. What is so disturbing about that? These are your assets, and you are entitled to give them to whoever you choose, with some limitations to prevent your spouse and children from being real life participants in a Charles Dickens story.

Wills can be simple "statutory" wills designed by state legislatures that are bare bones fill-in-the-blank documents sometimes available on-line or at public libraries. Like used Ford Pintos, it is better than nothing. But wills can also be overly complex documents that weigh enough to be used as ballast on an aircraft carrier. If a lawyer is charging you by the pound to prepare a will, find another attorney.

In this chapter, three issues involving wills are addressed:
- Dying without a will
- Common will provisions
- Pour-over wills

1. DYING WITHOUT A WILL

When a person dies without a will, state law governs who receives the estate. You would hope that losing control of your hard-earned assets would motivate people to have a will prepared. Sadly, this is not true.

According to the 2020 annual survey done by Caring.com, only 32% of the people who responded had a will. What is worse is that the percentage of survey participants without a will was 42% in their 2017 survey. In just three years, 25% more people have decided to let their state legislatures allocate their assets for them upon their death.

If you are among the nearly 70% of Americans who die without a will, you run the risk of dying intestate or dying to see which of your relatives will prevail in the Legislative Lotto which is the default option for will haters.

Should you believe that politicians are more capable than you to decide who should inherit your assets and in what amounts, then dying without a will is the right choice. Most people, however, do not have that same level of confidence in their elected officials and would prefer to make their own decisions on beneficiaries and the amounts they receive from your estate.

Certain assets like jointly held property avoid intestate transfers. Most of the accounts and methods discussed in Chapter 20 to bypass probate will also not be subject to intestacy transfers. Besides jointly held assets, properly completed beneficiary designations on life insurance, retirement plans, IRAs, bank accounts, etc. can effectively transfer assets. While these options avoid intestate transfers, they have their own set of potential pitfalls.

In one state (Michigan), if you die without a will leaving a spouse and descendants of you and your spouse, the following distribution of your intestate property takes place: 1) Your spouse inherits the first

$100,000 of your intestate property; 2) Your spouse receives one half (1/2) of the balance; and 3) Your descendants inherit everything else. Will your surviving spouse be OK with your children possibly receiving some of your assets prior to your spouse's death?

Again in Michigan, if you die without a will and are survived by a spouse and parents, your spouse will inherit the first $150,000 of your intestate property, plus ¾ of the balance. Your parents receive the rest. Do you parents need the funds more than your spouse? Upon the death of your parents, some of your funds might transfer to beneficiaries designated by your parents, not by you. Think of your least favorite brother who owes you money and his fourth wife. Is that outcome acceptable to you?

Wills are dead instruments. They give no one any authority to act until the maker/testator of the will is dead. Health care update: You can be severely ill and/or disabled more than once in your lifetime but you can only die once. That is why a good estate plan has not only a will, but durable powers of attorney (POAs) for financial matters and health care along with a revocable living trust. These other documents are discussed in upcoming Chapters 24 and 25.

Unlike a revocable trust, a will goes through probate. But as we discussed in Chapter 19, there are two types of probate: supervised probate and simplified probate.

Supervised probate can become the Nightmare on Dutch Elm Street horror movie with family members fighting for years, egged on by aggressive probate trial lawyers who will gladly stay in the fight as long as family members can pay their hourly rates.

Simplified probate (also known as independent or unsupervised probate) is handled at the counter of the courthouse as opposed to in front of a probate judge. Simplified probate is much cheaper, much quicker and frequently results in actually having some estate assets left to distribute to beneficiaries who are still speaking with each other years later.

EXAMPLE 1: Sue and John have been married for several years and have three grown children. They do not have wills because all of their assets are jointly held. John dies suddenly from a stroke. Sue is suffering from dementia and therefore cannot sign a will. Sue dies with all of her assets (her house, bank accounts, etc.) in her sole name. Probate will likely be required to transfer the assets to her three children.

Wills can be drafted to state that if probate is required, then simplified probate is to be used. Attorneys will sometimes write wills which say the opposite, that supervised probate is the preferred. Approach. Preferred by who? Why should it be automatically assumed that a judge and lawyers are needed to transfer assets? For a hefty fee, all trial attorneys who agree supervised probate is the best approach, please hold up your wallets.

2. COMMON WILL PROVISIONS

The primary purpose of a will is to help transfer your assets after you die.

In addition to designating who receives your assets, wills also usually include provisions like: 1) Naming who you want as your personal representative/executor; 2) Designating a guardian for your minor children; and 3) Indicating who should receive your personal property as well as the rest of your assets.

Personal representatives or executors are the individuals or institutions (trust companies) that you designate to administer your will. In this book, we will use the term personal representative since it is more modern. Whoever you select as your personal representative needs to be capable of carrying out your wishes and instructions while complying with local probate rules and regulations.

Name someone as your personal representative who is good at handling paperwork and forms. Nothing moves in the probate process without the required form. The same is true with filing claims for death benefits with insurance companies and retirement plan administrators. It is a waste of time to complain about the forms that are requested. Name someone who will either prepare the forms themselves or hire someone to do it for them.

You can name more than one person to act as personal representative. If you do, they are called co-personal representatives.

Be careful about naming multiple parties to serve as co-personal representatives. While two (or three) heads are supposedly better than one, what happens if they do not all agree?

In addition to naming your personal representative(s), if you have minor children, your will is where you normally nominate people to act as the guardians of your children. This frequently is a very emotional decision. Our experience is that the first choice of who you want as the guardian of your children is usually relatively easy. But the excitement starts when you are asked: "Who would be your next choice as guardian if your first choice is unable to act?"

If you name a couple to be co-guardians of your minor children, what happens if one co-guardian dies or the couple becomes divorced? Are you comfortable with only one of the named co-guardians acting alone? Would you want your brother-in-law to be sole guardian if your sister died? Make sure you have alternates as guardians and if you name couples as co-guardians, specify what happens if they are no longer a couple.

EXAMPLE 2: Sue and John are married with two young children. They have wills prepared naming each other as personal representatives with Sue's sister and John's father, in that order, as the alternate personal representatives. Sue and John name Sue's sister as the guardian of any of their children who are minors at the time of the death of the surviving spouse. The wills provide that the surviving spouse will inherit all the assets owned by Sue and John. After the death of the surviving spouse, the assets transfer in equal shares to their children. If both Sue and John have died and any of their surviving children are minors, then the share for that minor child will be held in a testamentary trust until spent or until the child turns 25.

Some people insist on listing in their wills all of the personal items they want given and to whom. While you may think which child gets your frequently thrown golf clubs and who gets your framed college degree is important, let your family decide which of your personal items they want. Include a method (lottery, etc.) to resolve disputes.

For expensive items like jewelry, designate who receives what on a list that is referenced in your will. It is much easier to change a list signed and dated by you than it is to change the will.

As previously written, it is not a good practice to transfer personal items by placing post-it notes on the back of the item which indicates who gets it. Who would ever switch the sticky note on the framed print by Don Van Go with the Picasso your grandfather bought in Spain 70 years ago?

3. POUR OVER WILLS

When a person signs a revocable trust, they usually also sign a pour-over will. A pour-over will transfer assets to a trust when the testator dies. Think of a pour-over will as a sweep document. A provision of the pour-over will say something like: "All the rest, residue and remainder of my estate I hereby transfer" to the previously executed trust.

Individuals with revocable trusts might forget they have certain assets in their sole name and never transfer them into their trust. Surviving spouses who had joint bank accounts with their spouse sometimes neglect to retitle those accounts. The pour-over can transfer assets into the trust, but it requires additional effort and paperwork which could be avoided.

EXAMPLE 3: Steven Jones executes a revocable self-trusteed trust on 10/24/2019. He also signs a pour-over will on the same day. In addition to naming personal representatives and designating who is to receive his personal property, the pour-over will has a provision which states: "I give all other property that I own to the trustee of the Steven Jones Trust Dated 10/24/2019, the terms of which are contained in a separate written document signed by me today, to be held, administered, and distributed under its terms as it exists at my death." This provision therefore acts to "pour-over" to Steven's self-trusteed trust those assets which were not already transferred prior to Steven Jones's death.

Pour-over wills are a fallback option to transfer assets to your revocable trust after your death. The better approach is to "fund" your trust during your lifetime so no probate, even independent probate, is required. Transfers of your assets to your trust which are easily accomplished by you are a lot more difficult by people acting on your behalf using a will or a POA. This is one time the old saying is correct: If you want something done right, do it yourself.

CHAPTER SUMMARY

Unless you have a trust, the primary purpose of a will is to indicate who you want to receive your assets after your death as opposed to having state law determine those distributions. Wills designate not only who receives what but also names a personal representative/executor to coordinate the transfer of your assets and guardians for any of your minor children. When you have a revocable trust, a pour over will is used to transfer assets into your trust which were in your sole name when you died.

TAKE ACTION

- Prepare and sign a will even if it is only a basic statutory will authorized by your state. Indicate who is to receive your personal property and other assets after your death.
- In your will, besides naming beneficiaries of your assets, designate your choices for personal representative/executor along with who you would want as potential guardians of your minor children.
- Execute a pour-over will if you have a revocable trust to make sure any assets that were not placed in your trust during your lifetime are "poured-over" to your trust after your death.

Chapter 24 – Trusts

"A trustee has a responsibility to guard the assets of others with a higher degree of care than he does his own."
John Ashcroft

CHAPTER PREVIEW

A trust is a third document you need as part of your estate plan to TRANSFER your wealth.

A trust is usually the longest and frequently the most important document in an estate plan. More than just a written document, a trust is a separate legal entity. Think of it as a company which can own assets like bank accounts, investments, real estate, etc. and you own the company.

The person who sets up a trust is called by a variety of names including settlor, grantor or trust maker. In the trust document, the settlor/grantor/maker names a trustee to administer the trust assets for the use and enjoyment of one or more beneficiaries.

In this chapter, the following three types of trusts will be discussed:
- Self-trusteed revocable living trusts
- Irrevocable trusts
- Testamentary trusts

1. SELF-TRUSTEED REVOCABLE LIVING TRUSTS

People frequently are opposed to having trusts because they believe that putting assets in a trust will result in their losing control of the assets. That is a really outdated concept.

The vast majority of trust documents signed today are called "self-trusteed revocable living trusts." In a self-trusteed trust, if you are the settlor/grantor/maker, you name yourself as the initial trustee and therefore you are wearing two hats. First, you are the maker (settlor or grantor) of the trust. Second, you are naming yourself as the initial trustee of your trust which is why it is "self-trusteed." Third, the settlor/grantor/maker of a self-trusteed trust usually name themselves as the beneficiary of the trust while they are alive which makes it a "living" trust.

The question people logically ask is why do I need to be wearing multiple hats?

Self-trusteed trust documents usually have a provision which says if the initial trustee (that would be you) is unable or unwilling to act, then the successor trustee(s) named by you step in and serve as trustee in your place. As the beneficiary of the trust, all assets in the trust have to be administered by the trustee (initial or successor) for your benefit during your lifetime and in particular if you are subsequently unable to handle your own financial affairs (due to a stroke, Alzheimer's, etc.)

As individuals get older and health issues become more of a concern, this ability to designate who is to manage your trust assets for your benefit during your lifetime becomes extremely important. This is the primary reason people will establish self-trusteed, revocable living trusts and put bank accounts, investments, real estate, etc. into their self-trusteed trusts during their lifetime.

EXAMPLE 1: John Smith is the settlor/grantor/maker of his self-trusteed trust which he signed on 3/10/2019. He names himself as the original trustee (self-trusteed). John names his spouse, Mary Smith as his first successor trustee and his oldest son, Robert Smith as his alternate successor trustee if Mary is also unable to act. John registers his investment account in the name of the trust as: "John Smith, Trustee of the John Smith Trust dated 3/10/2020." John manages his investment account until he has a stroke several years later. At that time, without court involvement, Mary takes over as trustee and manages the account for John's benefit. When John dies, the funds transfer to the beneficiaries named in his trust without going through probate.

Remember that any asset in the trust has to be used for the beneficiaries of the trust which is initially the settlor/grantor/maker.

The need for self-trusteed trusts is especially important for people who are single. Whether a surviving spouse or someone who has never married, a self-trusteed trust allows you to have control of your trust assets as long as you can properly manage them. But in the event of illness, incapacity or reduced ability to handle your own financial affairs, you decide (not the local probate court) as to who is to manage your assets for your benefit.

A surviving spouse frequently decides to place bank accounts, investments, etc. in joint name with a family member. This could cause major problems.

Jointly held assets could be involved in a child's divorce proceedings when they have to disclose all assets that they hold in sole or joint name. What happens if the child on the joint accounts dies in a car accident before the surviving spouse? Since accounts held jointly with rights of survivorship flow to the survivor upon the death of a joint holder, the funds will bypass a will or trust and could circumvent an intended distribution to all surviving children.

2. IRREVOCABLE TRUSTS

A revocable trust (described above) can be modified (amended) and/or revoked as long as the settlor/grantor/maker has the mental capacity to sign documents. An irrevocable trust normally cannot be revoked or changed. There are limited circumstances when an irrevocable trust can be changed but those options are best discussed with an estate planning attorney.

A revocable trust becomes irrevocable upon the incapacity or death of the settlor/grantor/maker of the trust. If you have suffered a stroke and are incapacitated, your document become irrevocable so that someone cannot have you change the beneficiaries of your trust when you do not fully comprehend what you are signing. The same is true after you die. The terms of your trust become irrevocable since only you had the ability to modify or revoke your trust during your lifetime.

An irrevocable trust which is irrevocable when it is signed is usually done to safeguard assets. A person can shelter assets in certain types of irrevocable trusts if they are willing to give up control.

EXAMPLE 2: Heather is single and a doctor. Heather wants to safeguard a portion of her assets in the event she remarries or is the target of a lawsuit. Heather establishes an irrevocable asset protection trust. During her lifetime, she will receive income from the trust. She will have limited control of the trust assets which must be used exclusively for her benefit during her lifetime. At the time of her death, the assets transfer to her nieces and nephews and her favorite charities.

While irrevocable asset protection trusts can shield assets from lawsuits, is the loss of control worth settling one up and funding it? Do you have substantial assets that could be taken in a lawsuit? Are you in a high-risk profession or a business owner who is concerned about being sued? While the maker of an irrevocable asset protection trust can retain very limited control over the administration of the trust, exercising what is determined to be too much authority will put the assets in play.

Not all estate planning attorneys have the credentials to draft irrevocable asset protection trusts. If you think you might need one, make sure the attorney you hire has the expertise needed to keep the trust assets secure from lawsuits.

Irrevocable insurance trusts were more popular when estate taxes were imposed at much lower levels. A person would create an irrevocable trust and then an independent trustee would purchase a life insurance policy with trust assets. Upon the death of the maker of the irrevocable trust, the life insurance proceeds would be payable to the trust. Because the life insurance policy was owned by the trust and not the deceased, the death benefit was not reduced by federal estate taxes since they were not included in the estate of the deceased maker of the irrevocable trust. Now that individuals can shelter $11,700,000 from federal estate taxes, in 2021 (Chapter 12), the need for irrevocable life insurance trusts has declined greatly.

3. TESTAMENTARY TRUSTS

A testamentary trust is a trust written as part of a will as in last will and "testament." Since wills are dead instruments that activate only after you have died, a testamentary trust inside a will cannot provide you with the living benefits available in a revocable trust.

Testamentary trusts can be named the "contingent" beneficiary of life insurance when minor children might otherwise receive the benefits. This is frequently the case with parents of minor children who have large amounts of life insurance through their employer but do not feel the need to have a revocable trust prepared at this time because their health is good, and they have other expenses that need to be addressed.

EXAMPLE 3: Sue and John are married and have four minor children. Both Sue and John work at companies where they purchase supplemental life insurance. Since they are young and healthy, Sue and John decide not to have trusts prepared at this time. Each of their wills contain a testamentary trust. If both Sue and John die and their surviving children are minors, their substantial life insurance death benefits will be held in the testament trust for the benefit of their children until each child reaches age 25. Sue and John name John's brother as the trustee of the testamentary trusts with Sue's mother as the successor trustee if John's brother is unable or unwilling to act.

Unlike revocable and irrevocable trusts, a testamentary trust requires probate administration but that by itself should not automatically disqualify the testamentary trust as a useful document. Make sure your will indicates that you want independent probate as opposed to the more expensive supervised probate if probate is involved. Your personal representative/executor can request supervised probate if circumstances require the involvement of a probate judge.

Always check with your employer to see if you have access to a legal services plan. MetLife and ARAG are two such plans. These plans usually cover the cost of wills, powers of attorney and in some cases revocable trusts. If you have minor children and you do not have coverage through your plan for a revocable trust, try to have a testamentary trust prepared and included in your covered will.

CHAPTER SUMMARY

Self-trusteed revocable living trusts are an especially important estate planning document as individuals become older and more concerned about health issues. Irrevocable trusts can be previously revocable trusts where the make has become incapacitated or has died. An irrevocable trust can also be used as an instrument to safeguard assets, but it requires giving up some control of the trust and trust assets. Testamentary trusts are part of a will and are frequently used to manage life insurance proceeds for minor children when both parents have died.

TAKE ACTION

- Sign a self-trusteed revocable living trust when you have assets, and you begin to be concerned about what would happen if you became incapacitated and could no longer manage your finances. Designate at least two successor trustees so if one is unable to act, you, not the probate court, have decided who should act as the trustee of your trust.
- Have an irrevocable trust prepared and sign it when you have substantial assets, and you are worried about being a target of a lawsuit or if you are in a high-risk profession. Consider signing an irrevocable life insurance trust if you are fortunate to have substantial wealth which could be subject to federal estate taxes.
- Include a testamentary trust in your will if you have minor children who might receive your assets if you are married and both you and your spouse are not alive.

Section Three: Create Your Legacy

Chapter 25 – Heir Pains

"Leave your children enough money so they can do anything, but not enough that they don't have to do anything."
Warren Buffet

CREATE YOUR LEGACY

Section Three on how to TRANSFER your wealth explains how to CREATE YOUR LEGACY by making distributions to: 1) Your heirs; 2) Charities directly; and 3) Charitable options for future donations.

CHAPTER PREVIEW

Distributing your wealth to your heirs is the most common way you create a legacy.

When a married person dies, most people leave all or the majority of their assets to their surviving spouse. When there is no surviving spouse, the assets are usually given to the children of the deceased. If there is no surviving spouse and a child of the deceased has died leaving children (grandchildren of the deceased), then it is common to have the share that would have gone to a deceased child be split between the children of a deceased child (grandchildren of the deceased).

EXAMPLE 1: John and Sue are married and have children and grandchildren. When John dies, he leaves his assets to his wife, Sue. When Sue dies, her estate plan transfers her assets to her "descendants." Depending on the language used, this usually means that Sue's children will divide her assets equally. But since one of Sue's daughters (Mary) died before Sue, the share that would have gone to Mary is now divided equally between Mary's children who are Sue's grandchildren.

The above example sounds pretty straight-forward. If only life and death were so simple. More Americans are preferring not to get married and 50% of Americans who do marry get divorced, sometimes remarry and have children by previous marriages. Plus, an increasing number of people are getting remarried much later in life after the death of a spouse. The profile of America now more closely resembles the TV sitcom "Modern Family" rather than "Leave It To Beaver." Hopefully, "The Addams Family" will not become the new normal.

Regardless of who you name as the beneficiaries of your estate, you have to decide if you want to leave your funds outright to your heirs or if the assets should be held in a trust with restrictions on how the funds can be spent. Warning: one sure way to have your heirs plant crabgrass on your grave is to place excessive limitations on how an inheritance can be spent.

In this chapter, we will examine ways to transfer assets to the following individuals:
- Your surviving spouse
- Your children and grandchildren
- Your parents and relatives

1. YOUR SURVIVING SPOUSE

While a large majority of married couples leave all their assets upon the death of one spouse to their surviving spouse, there are several ways to accomplish these transfers.

Jointly Held Assets

Most married couples own their checking, savings and investment accounts jointly in the names of both spouses. Married couples also usually own their home and other real estate jointly. As previously discussed in Chapter 20 (Avoiding Probate), jointly held accounts usually (but not always) have rights of survivorship. For jointly held assets between married individuals, upon the death of one spouse, the surviving spouse usually owns the assets with no restrictions.

Transferring assets to a surviving spouse is very easy by using joint ownership. The problem is that you have no way of knowing what the health of your surviving spouse will be at the time of your death. Nor do you know what will happen to the funds after your death.

EXAMPLE 2: Dave and Virginia are married and have children. This is the first marriage for each of them. Their assets are held jointly so when Dave dies, Virginia receives all the assets. Jack, a widower who is an old friend of Virginia and Dave dates and marries Virginia. Like many married couples, Virginia and Jack put their assets in joint accounts. Virginia dies first and the joint assets transfer to Jack. Since Jack's estate plan leaves his assets to his children from his first marriage, when Jack dies, the assets he received from Virginia now transfer to his children. Dave and Virginia's children receive nothing.

Be careful how you own assets. While putting assets in joint names to avoid probate is a viable option (Chapter 20), there are other ways to transfer assets to your spouse that you should at least consider.

Marital Trusts

Some married individuals, rightly or wrongly, feel that their spouses cannot handle money or might act impudently if they inherit funds without restrictions. In those cases, a person could set up their own trust (as opposed to or having all assets in joint name or in a joint trust) and direct that upon their death, funds would be administered by a trustee for the benefit of the surviving spouse.

This is a difficult decision and one that is very likely to cause hard feelings when a spouse learns that he or she will not have 100% control over their spouse's funds when their spouse dies. Some people avoid telling their spouse what they plan to do which always excites the estate planning attorney who gets to explain the terms of the trust of the deceased.

EXAMPLE 3: Carol and Fred are married with three adult children, one of whom, Cindy has serious problems with drugs and alcohol. Fred is concerned that if he dies before Carol, then Cindy will try to take advantage of her mother and to get money that Fred has always denied Cindy. Fred maintains substantial assets in joint name with Carol which will be under the control of whichever spouse survives the other. Fred, however, also has an investment account registered in the name of his trust which, upon his death will be held in a trust for the benefit of Carol. The trustees (Fred and Carol's sons) are authorized to pay funds for Carol's benefit, not Cindy's. Upon Carol's death, any remaining funds in the trust for Carol's benefit will be distributed to Fred and Carol's descendants with the portion for Cindy to be held as a discretionary trust to provide supplemental medical care and financial support to Cindy.

Obviously, most spouses are not happy to learn that their husband or wife does not feel they are capable of handling money, even if it is true. But leaving funds in trust for a surviving spouse (or child) is an option that should be considered if there are concerns about overbearing children, relatives or friends that could take advantage of a surviving spouse who otherwise would have sole ownership and control over substantial assets.

In addition to jointly held accounts, assets like IRAs, life insurance and annuities can be payable to the surviving spouse with a beneficiary designation. Other assets, like an investment account owned only by one spouse, can be paid to the surviving spouse without going through probate by using designations like payable on death (POD) or in trust for (ITF). Similar to jointly held assets, the surviving spouse receives these funds with no restrictions upon the death of the owner/spouse. But unlike jointly held assets, a sole owner is exactly that – the only owner. During the lifetime of the owner of the account, non-owner access to the account or asset is not available without a power of attorney (Chapter 22) or by an individual appointed by a court.

Blended families (second and third marriages)

In addition to concerns about spouses who might not be able to handle money, how to provide for spouses from a second or third marriage obviously is a major challenge for estate planners.

With over fifty percent of all marriages in the United States ending in divorce, blended families are becoming much more common. So how do you leave funds for your current spouse when you die but not disinherit your children from a prior marriage?

After your death, your surviving spouse might marry one of your fraternity brothers who you have not seen in over 30 years (true story). At last count, the fraternity brother was married to wife number five.

Most married clients in their first marriage leave their assets to their surviving spouse. While this happens in most first marriages, the estate plans of people married two or three times is obviously more complicated. Over 50% of all marriages in the United States end in divorce so the issue of transferring your wealth to your heirs is becoming more complex. Plus, people are living longer so the prospect of second and third marriages for widows and widowers is becoming more common as well.

How do you provide for your current spouse and make sure that children from a prior marriage receive something from your estate?

Some people will leave funds for charities which is the subject of Chapter 26. Others have no children or grandchildren, so they provide funds for family and friends which is covered later in this Chapter.

EXAMPLE 4: Cathy and Peter are a married couple. Both of them were previously married and each have two grown children from their first marriages. Cathy and Peter own a house together with a relatively large mortgage balance. They each want to provide for each other when they die but also want to make sure that a portion of their respective estates ultimately flow to their children from the prior marriage. Cathy and Peter each create a QTIP trust naming their surviving spouse as the beneficiary. As required by Federal law, all income from the QTIP trust must be paid to the surviving spouse. Principle from the trust can be paid to the surviving spouse if need is proven to the satisfaction of the independent trustee. Upon the death of the surviving spouse, any remaining funds in the trust are paid to the children of the maker/settlor of the QTIP trust. The result is that the surviving spouse has income and potential access to trust principle for living expenses and to pay the mortgage, but the children of the maker/settlor will ultimately receive whatever is left in the QTIP trust.

2. CHILDREN AND GRANDCHILDREN

Congratulations if you have perfect children and grandchildren who all are in the running to win the Nobel Prize for Economics before they turn 30. However, most parents and grandparents are not so fortunate. Sometimes parents and grandparents decide to place restrictions on inheritances until the beneficiaries each reach a certain age when they will hopefully be more responsible. Unfortunately, unlike fine wines and expensive cheeses, children and grandchildren do not always improve with age.

EXAMPLE 5: Valerie and Phil are married with four children, three of whom are children. Valerie and Phil believe their children are all responsible enough to manage any funds they inherit so upon the death of the surviving spouse, their then surviving children will divide their estate equally. In the event one of the three children predecease the surviving spouse and that deceased child has children (Valarie and Phil's grandchildren) then the one-fourth share that would have gone to the deceased child could be held in trust for the benefit of the grandchildren by that parent.

Parents need to decide if their children and grandchildren can manage money currently and if not, then at what age should the funds be distributed to them? Some people will make the distribution at age 25, some at 30 or any age they determine is suitable.

If the funds for children or grandchildren are held in trust for their benefit, then it is important to know that the funds are not frozen in most trusts. The trustee of the trust can be authorized to pay from the trust for a beneficiary, living expenses, education costs, health care, the down payment on a house, etc. Funds are not frozen unless the trust document you had prepared locks up the funds until the beneficiary reaches a particular age.

EXAMPLE 6: Anita and Paul are married with three children, one of whom, Theresa is autistic. Theresa is currently receiving disability payments from Social Security because she is unable to work and has few assets. Anita and Paul contact an elder care attorney who prepares a special needs trust for Theresa that will receive funds when both Anita and Paul have died. The trustee of the special needs trust is instructed to supplement the care that Theresa receives from other sources. Since the special needs trust is the owner of the assets, they are not included in calculations to determine if Theresa has too many assets and income to qualify for assistance.

3. PARENTS AND RELATIVES

People who do not have children will frequently leave funds to parents. When leaving funds for parents, you need to consider what will happen to those funds when your parent dies. Will your funds intended to support your parents transfer to your parent's beneficiaries or ones you select?

When your parents die, their estate plans, not your plan controls the distribution of their assets.

Think of that lazy brother-in-law that you cannot stand. If you leave funds for your mother, when she dies, your mother divides her estate equally between her children and grandchildren. The share for your sister will make Bubba your brother-in-law extremely happy once he finally wakes up.

Consider creating a discretionary trust for the benefit of parents and grandparents. Upon your death, you allocate funds to a trust naming your parents as discretionary beneficiaries. The trustee of the discretionary trust is directed to use the trust funds to supplement whatever government benefits (if any) your parents and grandparents receive. Upon the death of the last beneficiary/parent, whatever funds are left transfer according to your wishes, not those of your parents.

EXAMPLE 7: Tom's mother, Ann is a widow who has major health issues. Tom decides to leave a portion of his assets in a discretionary trust for the benefit of Ann as opposed to leaving funds outright to her. The trust supplements whatever care Ann receives from government sources like Medicaid. When Ann dies or if she fails to survive Tom, the funds in the trust are divided equally between Tom's children.

If you decide to leave funds to relatives like sisters, brothers, nieces and nephews, you have to think about what happens if one of those named relatives has died before you. Does the share that would have gone to your deceased brother drop down to his children, your nieces and nephews? Or is the share divided proportionately between the surviving named relatives?

An experienced estate planning attorney will help you plan for different outcomes without drafting documents that make War and Peace look like a short story. Never pay an attorney by the word or by what the document weighs.

CHAPTER SUMMARY

Surviving spouses are the most frequent beneficiaries of jointly held assets when the first spouse dies. With an increasing number of people getting married a second or third time and having children from a prior marriage, it is becoming more common to have some of the funds of a deceased spouse placed in a QTIP trust for the limited use of the surviving spouse and ultimate transfer to the children of the first marriage. Children and grandchildren are usually next in the transfer line after surviving spouses. Grandchildren will frequently inherit the share that would have gone to one of their parents who died prior to the death of their father or mother (the grandparent of a beneficiary). Parents and other relatives sometimes are beneficiaries if the deceased is single and has no children or grandchildren. Funds for parents could be placed in a discretionary trust to supplement expenses not covered by other sources.

TAKE ACTION

- If you are married, take a very objective look at options to leave assets to your spouse. This is especially important if this is your second or third marriage and you have children by a prior marriage. Explore options like QTIP trusts but be honest with your spouse about what you ultimately put into place to transfer assets to them and restrictions that might result.
- Decide if your children and grandchildren are currently capable of handling a potential inheritance. If you feel they are too young or have difficulty managing money responsibly, leave their inheritance in a trust until they reach a particular age.
- Review your parents' financial situation. Determine if it would be appropriate to leave any funds they might receive from you in a trust as opposed to distributing the money to them without any restrictions. Any funds you leave outright to your parents will be transferred according to their estate plans, not yours at the time of their death.

Chapter 26 – Selecting Charities

*"If you haven't got any charity in your heart,
you have the worst kind of heart trouble."*
Bob Hope

CHAPTER PREVIEW

*Making gifts directly to selected charities is a second way to create
your legacy when you TRANSFER your wealth.*

Once you have provided for your spouse, your children, your
parents and anyone else you feel you need to support, consider
creating a legacy of doing good for people in need. Giving to charities
can be done during your lifetime or after you have died. The amount
you give is far less important than trying to make sure your donations
will accomplish the positive impact you seek.

Due to recent changes in Federal income tax laws, the standard
deduction for individuals was doubled. Fewer individuals benefit
from itemizing deductions, including donations to charities. While
there is always a need to support good charities, the recent decline in
charitable donations has negatively impacted charities at a time when
COVID demands are increasing.

In this chapter, three aspects of charitable giving are addressed:
- Make a difference
- Check before you give
- Contribute your time

In upcoming Chapter 27 (Charitable Ways to Give) we will review
different options you have to make contributions to charities. But you
first have to decide the causes that you are passionate about, and
which charities conduct programs which effectively support those
causes.

1. MAKE A DIFFERENCE

Americans are extremely generous. An estimated $449.64 billion was donated to U.S. charities in 2019 by American individuals, bequests, foundations and corporations according to Giving USA, a public service initiative of The Giving Institute.

Charitable giving is not dominated by the mega-wealthy according to an article in The Wall Street Journal of 1/9/2020: "The lion's share of America's vast philanthropy comes from ordinary citizens, 100 million of whom make charitable gifts annually, with an average household donating around $3,000. In addition, 77 million citizens volunteer time and labor. This broad generosity powers some 1.5 million independent nonprofits across the country".

When deciding what charities to support, first determine what you are passionate about.

Do images of long lines at food banks make you want to send a check to that charity? Did you lose a parent, relative or close friend to cancer or some other disease? Have you benefited professionally from going to a college or university that provided you financial aid to help you complete your education? Then consider contributing to the college you attended or to a charity that supports the causes you believe in.

EXAMPLE 1: Cheryl is the first person in her immediate family to graduate from college. Cheryl worked part-time while attending classes and her parents contributed whatever they could afford to give her for her tuition and books. Cheryl applied for and received a limited number of scholarships from the college she attended which was critical to her completing her degree. Having recently retired after a successful career, Cheryl has decided to donate to a scholarship fund at the college she graduated from to enable other students to enjoy the financial success she has achieved.

The COVID-19 pandemic has put millions of Americans out of work. There is no shortage of need. Help fill the funding gap and make a difference in someone's life.

2. CHECK BEFORE YOU GIVE

When you contribute to a charity, how do you know that your donation is going to carry out the programs you support rather than being spent on extensive marketing and above average executive salaries?

It is hard to believe that some people are so unethical that they would set up phony charities to divert money to themselves. Unfortunately, it happens all too often. Some charities close and then reopen under another name with the same goal to take in contributions from well-intended individuals and distribute the funds to themselves or family members providing "marketing services' to the charity at inflated prices.

Fortunately, there are organizations which rate the effectiveness of charities based on information reported in the tax returns 501 (c) (3) charities have to file with the IRS every year. Failure to file the required returns could result in the loss of tax-exempt status so most charities comply even if it means disclosing information that confirms that a very small percentage of the funds, they raise goes to benefit those people or causes they claim to help.

Some of the organizations which rate charities are:

Charity Navigator   charitynavigator.org
Charity Watch   charitywatch.org
GuideStar   guidestar.org

EXAMPLE 2: Barb's mother died after a long battle with cancer. Barb recently received a solicitation in the mail for a group claiming to provide funds for cancer treatment for low-income cancer patients in rural communities similar to the one where her mother lived and died. Before she contributes, Barb looks up the charity on GuideStar and discovers that only 20% of the millions they raise actually goes to cancer related programs. The other 80% goes for fundraising and for high salaries for their executives. Barb instead donates to a different charity where 85% of the funds they raise go to help cancer patients.

Check before you contribute. Difficult times bring out the best and worst in people. Take the time to make sure your donations will be spent wisely.

3. CONTRIBUTE YOUR TIME

If you can, seek out charities that need your time as well as your money. There are food banks that could always use volunteers to stock shelves in their panty. Meals on Wheels needs people to deliver food to home-bound seniors and disabled individuals. Look and ask around. Spending time at a charity also enables you to witness how they operate and if they are effectively using donations to benefit those they claim to help.

For charities that are far from your home or in other countries, you could help host a fundraiser. You might help raise money for an orphanage in a less developed country that is supported by a local church. Or supporting an effort to raise money to provide clean drinking water to a village in a distant country.

You may not be wealthy in a financial sense, but your time has great value. Contribute wisely.

EXAMPLE 3: Bill loves to play golf and runs a golf league that plays once a week. Bill volunteers every year to help organize a golf outing that raises funds for a group which renovates houses for disabled veterans. Bill not only raises a substantial amount of money each year organizing an event involving his enjoyment of golf, but he also volunteers his time (and his golf buddies) to fix up homes used by disabled veterans. A great three for one deal.

CHAPTER SUMMARY

Americans support a great number of charities and there is no shortage of groups needing financial and volunteer help to support their causes. Organizations exist which rate charities based on how much of the money they raise goes for fundraising and how much goes for charitable programs. Donating money is important but so is contributing your time.

TAKE ACTION

- Make a list of the institutions and causes you are passionate about.
- Identify charities which support those causes and research how they are spending the money they raise. Eliminate charities where little goes for programs, and much is spent on administration, executive compensation and fundraising.
- Volunteer at a charity in your community which supports the causes you are passionate about. This is an excellent way to see how your donations are being spent.

Chapter 27 – Charitable Ways to Give

"We make a living by what we get,
but we make a life by what we give. "
Winston Churchill

CHAPTER PREVIEW

Utilizing IRS-approved giving options like donor advised funds, charitable trusts and IRA qualified charitable distributions is a third way to create your legacy as you TRANSFER your wealth.

Sending a check to a charity or charging a donation on a credit card are simple ways to support a particular charity you believe in. But besides sending a check, there are other options available to donate, receive a charitable deduction and still retain some control over your donation.

Maybe you want to eventually donate to certain charities however you currently need the income that your savings provide you. Or you have enough current income, you want to support a charity, but you are concerned that your children might not be able to put away enough for their retirement and will need the funds you would otherwise donate.

People frequently assume that you must have millions of dollars available to set up accounts that support charities but permits you to still have a say in how the funds are spent. While setting up a private foundation is complex and is rarely established for less than two million dollars, there are other options to give which can be implemented with relatively modest donations.

In this chapter, three options for charitable giving will be discussed:
- Donor advised funds
- Charitable trusts
- IRA Qualified Charitable Distributions

1. DONOR ADVISED FUND (DAF)

Instead of making a donation directly to a charity and hoping the funds are used as you intended, consider contributing funds in a manner that enables you to retain some degree of control. You might be concerned that a charity you support will change their mission or has begun to spend more on fundraising than helping people. A charity like a small church you attend, and support might close when it no longer has enough members to cover their operating expenses.

If you want to make a gift that qualifies as a charitable deduction, but you still want to retain some control over which charities benefit from your gift, consider establishing a donor advised fund (DAF).

A donor advised fund is a charitable account set up by someone (the donor) who contributes to the account. A donor advised fund is a separate account maintained by a larger charity which handles the administrative and reporting duties that charities are required to do in order to keep their non-profit status with the IRS.

The large charity assumes the responsibility for the complex reporting requirements for all the separate donor advised accounts under their administration. Having one charity coordinate reporting for several small charitable accounts greatly reduces operating expenses.

As the name implies, in a donor advised fund, the donor retains the ability to "advise" the larger charity as to how the funds in the separate account are to be used. The assets in a donor advised fund are usually invested in mutual funds until a donation recommended by the donor is approved and mailed to the charity. The term "donor advised" means that the administrative charity reserves the right to reject donation requests they feel would violate IRS guidelines.

Inappropriate requests include charitable gifts where the donor is receiving something of value from a charity in exchange for their donation which violates IRS regulations. The administrative charity is serving as the compliance department to ensure that the charity does not lose their non-profit status and can continue to provide cost-effective reporting services for DAFs under their umbrella.

EXAMPLE 1: Laura sets up a donor advised fund and contributes $8,000 to the fund. Laura receives a charitable deduction of $8,000 even though she did not designate which charities will ultimately receive the funds. After a major hurricane, Laura notifies the administrators of her donor advised fund that she wants to donate $100 from her DAF to the American Red Cross for disaster relief. The administrators of the charitable fund reviewed the request for a $100 grant and approved the gift after verifying that the charity was a non-profit registered with the IRS.

DAFs are extremely popular. According to 2020 Donor-Advised Fund Report by the National Philanthropic Trust, in 2019, there were 873,228 DAF accounts, an increase of 19.4% over 2018. Assets in DAFs in 2019 totaled $141.95 billion. Over $27.3 billion in grants were made from DAFs in 2019.

Having to obtain approval of their grant recommendations by a third party is viewed as a drawback for some people who are considering establishing a DAF. Individuals can always contribute directly to charities they want to support without going through a DAF. Given the popularity of DAFs and their increased use, the approval restrictions appear to be acceptable to a significant number of people who are charitably inclined and want to retain partial control over how the donations are made.

Three of the many institutions which offer donor advised funds are:

Fidelitycharitable.org   (800) 952-4438
Schwabcharitable.org   (800) 746-6216
Vanguardcharitable.org   (888) 383-4483

The flexibility of donor advised funds has been highlighted during the COVID pandemic. Grants are being directed to areas that donors feel have the greatest need given record high unemployment.

As reported in the August 2020 issue of Financial Advisor Magazine, "Grants made through Fidelity's donor advised fund to free food programs soared 667% during the first four months of 2020 from the same period in 2019. And in 38 states, giving to human services charities such as food banks and homeless shelters, topped the giving categories. In 2019 those charities were the top recipients in only six states, Fidelity said."

Fidelity and Schwab currently do not have a minimum investment amount to open a donor advised fund while Vanguard requires a minimum of $25,000. If a donor advised fund charges an annual fee of 0.6 percent (.6%) of the assets, then for a DAF with a balance of $10,000, you are paying fees of $60 per year to handle the recordkeeping and tax compliance. The investments available for DAF accounts have their own fees which are in addition to the administrative fees.

2. CHARITABLE TRUSTS

Sometimes a person wants to retain control over who receives future grants of their donated funds but does not want to give up authority to the administrators of a donor advised fund. An individual might want to receive a tax deduction today but still receive income from the donated funds for their lifetime.

In those cases, establishing charitable trust might be appropriate. Unlike a private foundation which usually requires a donation of at least one million dollars, certain types of charitable trusts can be created for far less dollars.

Although Donor Advised Funds (DAFs) have become very popular in recent years, some people are concerned that the charity operating the donor advised funds might not approve their requests. Donor "advised" means that the donor submits a request for a particular charity to receive a grant from the fund. If the charity staff does not feel the request is going to a charity approved by the IRS, they have the right and responsibility to deny the request.

Instead of a donor advised fund, individuals can establish a charitable fund where they are members of a board which votes on grants. The board assumes the decision-making responsibility that would have been given to the administrators of the donor advised fund.

The IRS has sample language available to create a simple charitable trust. In some cases, the donor wants to receive some type of benefit from their donation during their lifetime. The donor still receives a tax deduction, but it is usually not as great as an outright contribution.

In some cases, a person may want to receive income from a charity for the rest or her or his life with the principal going to the charity when the donor dies. This is the concept behind a Charitable Remainder Trust where the "Remainder" goes to the charity.

In other cases, a person wants a charity to have the income from a gift for a certain number of years. After the term ends, the funds that were providing income to the charity return to the donors or her or his family. This is called a Charitable Lead Trust.

While Charitable Remainder Trusts and Charitable Lead Trusts are discussed later in this chapter, private foundations are not since they usually make sense only for individuals prepared to donate at least one million. The complexity of private foundations is beyond the scope of this book.

Charitable Remainder Trusts

In a charitable remainder trust, a donor transfers funds to a trust which pays an amount to the donor or another family member for a fixed number of years or for a lifetime. At the end of the term or when the donor dies, the remaining principal goes to the charity.

EXAMPLE 2: Susana wants to donate to the college she graduated from but has a need for income in retirement so she cannot afford to make an outright gift to her school during her lifetime. She donates $10,000 to MSU which sets a charitable remainder trust. The trust will pay Susana $390 per quarter ($,560 per year} for the rest of her life. Susana receives a one-time tax deduction $2,203 which is based on her age. Upon her death, the balance of the $10,000 will be transferred to MSU.

Charitable Lead Trusts

Charitable lead trusts are the opposite of charitable remainder trusts. In this case, a donor permits a charity to receive the income from a pool of funds for a certain number of years. At the end of the term, say 10 years, the funds in the pool return to the donor or the donor's estate if the donor has died.

EXAMPLE 3: Dennis wants to support the university he attended but also wants to leave funds for his grandchildren. Dennis transfers $100,000 into a charitable lead trust which will last for 20 years. During the 20-year period, the income from the trust is paid to the university. At the end of the 20 years, the principal of the trust is paid to Dennis' grandchildren.

3. IRA QUALIFIED CHARITABLE DISTRIBUTIONS (QCD)

A relatively new way to give is to make charitable donations directly from your IRA. Called a Qualified Charitable Distribution (QCD), this can be a very useful option for older individuals who are required to take minimum distributions from their IRAs, are charitably inclined but also want to minimize their income tax liability.

Instead of taking funds from an IRA and paying tax on the amount withdrawn, a Qualified Charitable Deduction (QCD) is sent directly from an IRA to a charity. Because the IRA owner never receives the funds, the potential tax impact with a QCD is less than if the withdrawal went directly to the IRA owner who then made a donation to a charity.

Traditional IRAs are tax deferred. That means you usually receive an up-front income-tax deduction when you contribute to a traditional IRA. You may have rolled tax-deferred funds from an employer sponsored plan like a 401(k) or 403(b) when you left or retired from your previous employer. As you withdraw funds from your traditional IRA, the withdrawal is taxed as ordinary income.

Up until the Cares Act of 2020, when an IRA owner turned 70½, the account owner had to take a Required Minimum Distribution

(RMD) from their IRA or face a possible 50% (not a typo, 50%) penalty on the amount that should have been taken out. Currently, RMDs do not have to begin until the year an IRA owner turns 72.

While the law was changed to delay RMD's to age 72, the earliest date to take a Qualified Charitable Distribution (QCD) is still 70½. The opportunity is there but the tax incentive is not.

EXAMPLE 4: April is a widow who recently celebrated her 75th birthday. April and her deceased husband accumulated $500,000 in traditional IRAs of which April is now the owner. Since April is over 70½, and is subject to the previous RMD rule, she has to take a Required Minimum Distribution but does not really need the funds since she receives a pension, social security and has other income. Instead of receiving the RMD and having to report it as ordinary income, April directs her IRA custodian to contribute the RMD to her favorite charity. April does not receive a deduction for her gift, she does avoid paying the Medicare surcharge because her taxable income is not increased by the amount of the QCD. IRS rules prohibit a QCD to a donor advised fund (DAF). This might be because the IRS does not want the IRA owner to retain any control (even if limited) over the funds once they are transferred from the IRA to the designated charity.

The amount of the tax deduction and size of the quarterly payment depends on the age of the donor and interest rates at the time of the gift. If you are considering making a charitable gift involving a charitable trust, contact the charity first and ask for them to run sample proposals for you to review.

CHAPTER SUMMARY

Donor advised funds enable a person to receive an immediate tax deduction for a gift but then retain some control over which charities receive the funds over time. Assets in a donor advised funds can be invested and might grow over time to produce additional funds to gift. Charitable remainder trusts provide income to the donor or other designated individuals and then pass the remainder to a charity when the income beneficiaries have died. Charitable lead trusts allow the charity to use the donation for a certain number of years and then returns the funds to the donor. Qualified Charitable Distributions (QCDs) are an effective way to satisfy Required Minimum Distributions (RMDs) while benefiting your favorite charities. Distributions are made directly from an IRA to a charity so that some income tax surcharges are avoided.

TAKE ACTION

- To provide on-going donations to your favorite charities, establish a donor advised fund which can be opened for as little as $5,000 during your lifetime or after your death.
- Establish a Charitable Remainder Trust (CRT) If you want to receive an income tax deduction for a donation and receive income from a charity during your lifetime. Upon your death, your designated charity will receive the remaining fund in the CRT.
- Create a Charitable Lead Trust (CLT) to obtain a current income tax deduction while allowing a charity to have the income from the CLT for a certain number of years. At the end of the term, the principal of the CLT returns to you or your beneficiaries.
- If you are over 70 ½ and are planning to donate to a charity, consider making your donation to your favorite charity directly from your IRA. Depending on the relevant tax law, you might be able to satisfy your Required Minimum Distribution and avoid some additional surtaxes.

CONCLUSION

"How you start is important, but it is how you finish that counts. In the race for success, speed is less important than stamina. The sticker outlasts the sprinter."
B.C. Forbes

Start Your Journey

It does not matter if you are just starting to build wealth, you are trying to increase your assets prior to retirement or you need to reload your accounts following an economic setback like COVID 19.

Whatever the reason you decided to read this book, you need to set goals for yourself, establish a plan and act to Grow, Employ and Transfer (GET) Wealth.

A general goal might be to achieve financial independence. Great. Since it will probably be a long journey, what do you hope to accomplish by January 1 of the upcoming year? What about your goals 12 months from the upcoming January 1? What are you willing to do and willing to give up in order to accomplish those goals?

The Race For Success

Only you can define what success means to you. It might be having a certain amount of money when you retire, or it could be having your children all graduate from college with no student loans and be gainfully employed. Success for you might be having a modest paid off home that you are able to share with someone who you respect and enjoy spending time with.

However you define success, realize that you can always move the finish line just a little bit further. Never give up pursuing new goals. You will be a success because you made the effort.

Your journey starts right now. Take the first step.

Henry S. Woloson

ABOUT THE AUTHOR

Henry S. Woloson is currently the manager and founder of Woloson Financial Management, LLC located in Clarkston, Michigan. The company, which Henry owns along with his daughter, Laura, handles personal investments and offers securities and advisory services through Harbour Investments, Inc. Information about the investments and services they offer can be found on their website: www.WolosonFinancial.com.

In addition to being an investment advisor representative, Henry is a practicing attorney focusing on the preparation of estate planning documents such as trusts, wills and powers of attorney. More information about their estate planning services is available at: www.WolosonLegal.com.

Henry is thankful that he has been able to support several charities as a Board member of a private foundation and through several donor advised funds that he has help establish.

Prior to forming Woloson Financial Management, LLC, Henry worked for several years at a major national bank where he gained experience in trust services and investment management.

Henry S. Woloson received his BA in journalism from Wayne State University, his MA from Central Michigan University and his JD from Wayne State University Law School.

Henry welcomes your comments regarding this book and how future additions could be improved. He can be reached at henry@WolosonFinancial.com, henry@WolosonLegal.com or www.WolosonFinancial.com

Thank you.

Made in the USA
Columbia, SC
26 March 2023

14325356R00130